EUROPA ✠ MILITARIA
SPECIAL Nº6

THE
VIKINGS

RECREATED IN COLOUR PHOTOGRAPHS

BRITTA NURMANN, CARL SCHULZE
& TORSTEN VERHÜLSDONK

THE CROWOOD PRESS

This edition published in 1999 by
The Crowood Press Ltd
Ramsbury, Marlborough
Wiltshire SN8 2HR

www.crowood.com

This impression 2004

British Library Cataloguing-in-Publication Data
A catalogue record for this book is available from
the British Library.

ISBN 1 86126 289 2

Designed by Tony Stocks/TS Graphics

Printed and bound in Malaysia
by Times Offset (M) Sdn Bhd

Authors' acknowledgements
We would like to record our gratitude to all the
re-enactors and living history societies who
supported us, by word and deed, during the
preparation of this book, and all those who
kindly stood still while we took our pictures.
We cannot name these many individuals here,
but they know who they are. Special thanks are
due to Frank Wiedemann, who provided us
with background material and answered many
questions; to Miss Melanie Donus for supplying
additional photographic material; and to
Simone and Ivor Lawton of Dawn of Time
Crafts, 18 Anne Close, Brightlingsea,
Essex L07 OLS, UK, makers of early medieval
equipment for museums and re-enactment,
who kindly let us reproduce some of their
archive pictures.

CONTENTS

Preface

What do we know actually know about the Vikings? Between the 8th and the 11th centuries they travelled throughout Europe, to parts of North America and to the Middle East as traders, warriors and colonists. They were feared as enemies by every people they encountered. Yet we have much less reliable information about this group of Scandinavian peoples than we do about more ancient cultures such as Imperial Rome. Everything known to modern man about the Vikings is based on three types of sources: archaeological finds; written descriptions, which as a rule were not recorded by the Vikings themselves; and the Nordic sagas - originally oral traditions, usually written down for the first time in the 12th or 13th centuries.

From such major excavations as Haithabu, Moosgard, Birka, Roskilde, Lindholm Hoeje, Gokstad, Skuldelev, York and Gjermundbu we have abundant material remains which, when compared with the written evidence, cast light on many aspects of Viking culture, but which equally pose new questions. Mistaken interpretations, and a glorification of some specific aspects of the Viking era, have planted in the public mind an unbalanced picture of these peoples which fails to do them justice.

In this book we try to introduce readers to Viking culture by means of photographs taken at re-enactment displays mounted by Viking "living history" societies, to create a more intimate and human impression than they may gain from "dead" archaeological finds. We hope to correct, at least to some extent, the most ingrained of the mistaken ideas about these vigorous, creative peoples, and to give readers some insight into the period of European history when the Scandinavian nations were dominant.

These re-enactors go to considerable pains to achieve high levels of authenticity, taking into account all sources of information. The hobby of "living history" does not simply mean the exact reconstruction of known archaeological finds, but tries to bring a whole era back to life. Each re-enactor creates a character, taking into account all available knowledge and relevant finds; he or she reconstructs clothing and equipment which may not have been found by archaeologists in exactly that form, but which are typical for the period. Old crafts have been revived (especially where decorative elements are concerned), and new pieces have been made in styles which have been dead for many centuries.

This is a challenging task. For instance, the problems begin with the difficulty of obtaining the correct types of fabric for making clothing; this must be authentically spun into yarn, dyed, and woven into cloth. Re-enactors often seek to work as closely as possible with museums and archaeologists, but this is not easy - living history enthusiasts are rarely granted access to the finds which gather dust in the reserve collections of scholarly institutions.

Although necessary for building interest and acceptance of the hobby, the public shows at which re-enactors recreate authentic life present their own problems. Whereas a nearly perfect impression of, say, a craftsman might be possible if enough trouble were taken, a convincing impression of a Viking age skirmish will always fail because of the

(**Above**) From the 8th to the 11th century all Europe trembled before the Scandinavian sea-rovers who first ravaged the coasts and later invaded large areas in strength. Yet the Vikings were not mere looters; these most skilled seafarers of their age were also explorers, traders, and colonists seeking new homes at a time of exploding population in their relatively unproductive homelands. Today European re-enactors try to bring the Viking age alive again at their public performances, not only recreating the Viking warrior but also offering an insight into everyday life, crafts and trade.

necessary safety precautions. There are also few reconstructions of Viking age ships, for obvious reasons of cost and logistics.

Despite these problems the Viking re-enactment movement puts on numerous events all over Northern Europe every year, and succeeds in casting its spell over thousands of spectators. These are not merely light-hearted costumed pageants; they play an important part in correcting mistaken historical impressions, particularly among the young; and sometimes it even happens that the recreation and practical use of pieces of period equipment can answer questions for the historians.

The authors wish good luck to all the re-enactors whom we met during the assembly of material for this book; we made many friends among them. We also hope that the future may bring improved co-operation between living history re-enactors and historians and archaeologists, who have a great deal to offer one another in their mutual search for knowledge.

3

Introduction

In the old Norse tongue the word *viking* meant something like raiding or piracy, and *vikingr* meant a raider. Though today this word is used as a general term for the Nordic peoples of the 8th to 11th centuries, it was used more rarely in the early medieval period. Their fellow Europeans used to speak rather of "Norsemen" - men from the north (a term which lives on in "Norman", since Normandy was founded by Scandinavian colonists). The peoples of eastern Europe and the Balkans used the terms "Rus" and "Varangians" for the Norse invaders, traders, colonists and mercenaries.

Why did these Scandinavian peoples leave their homes from the late 8th century onwards, to plunder the coasts and river estuaries of Europe, and eventually to settle far away - as many did in England, Ireland, France and Russia? The main reason seems to have been overpopulation, leading to a severe shortage of land capable of sustaining their farming communities. Even in the valleys of these often mountainous and forested regions the soil was not particularly fertile. This period of hardship and want coincided with a Scandinavian mastery of seamanship outclassing that of all other European nations; so it was inevitable that many sought to improve their lot by raiding the richer Christian lands to the south.

At first these were summer raids, between seedtime and harvest, sporadic and limited in size. Later, spreading word of their success increased their numbers and frequency as raiders bore home silver, slaves, farm stock, and every other kind of booty. In order to dominate the targeted areas more thoroughly they took to wintering there in stockaded coastal camps. Later still, many were attracted by the fertile and ill-guarded lands they raided; they began to fetch over their families and goods to settle permanently. Norwegians and Danes sought new lands across the North Sea and the North Atlantic; the Swedes wandered down the great rivers into the huge Slavic wilderness of today's Russia.

The British Isles were greatly influenced by the Vikings. Only 72 years passed between the first recorded raid, on Lindisfarne by Norwegian Vikings in 793, and the founding of the Danelaw - an area of permanent Viking settlement which included most of the northern and eastern third of England. Although the Anglo-Saxons reconquered the Danelaw under King Edward the Elder in the years up to 924, Viking settlers still came to England. For example, it took the Saxons another 30 years to take back York, reconquered by King Eadred only in 954. In Ireland, too, though the Vikings were defeated in 902, many of today's Irish cities are Viking foundations.

By the mid-10th century, both in England and Ireland, many of the long-settled Vikings had converted from their pagan religion to Christianity; and as the centuries passed they merged their blood, and remnants of their language, with the earlier inhabitants. In today's Russia, and in the Carolingian Empire which then embraced much of France, the Low Countries and western Germany, the Viking settlers also mixed with the original populations.

Vikings who had converted to Christianity in their new homelands returned to Scandinavia with missionaries. These often began their efforts to convert the population by concentrating on the local kings - and often they succeeded. Some of these rulers had little difficulty in

persuading their peoples to convert to the new faith in their turn; others tried too abruptly and forcibly. (Olaf Tryggvasson's brutal missionary campaign in his kingdom of Norway cost him his life at the battle of Svoldr, where his fleet was defeated by an alliance of followers of the old gods.)

Unlike Denmark and parts of today's southern Sweden, which formed a kingdom early in the 8th century, Norway was forcibly united by Harald Finehair and was called a kingdom only from 900 onwards. Vikings who fled Harald's reign settled in Iceland, and formed a democracy under the so-called *allthing*, a gathering of all free men. Cnut the Great ("Canute"), who followed his father Svein Forkbeard on the throne of Norway in 1014, was king of England, Norway and Denmark. Coin finds show that the Swedish people may also have regarded this mightiest of the Viking kings as leader; but his kingdom broke up soon after his death in 1035.

Their swift, shallow-draught ships allowed the Vikings to cover long distances both on the high seas and up major rivers. As the navigational skills of the Scandinavian seafarers were superior to those of their contemporaries, they often appeared without warning, mounting surprise attacks straight from the edge of the water. Vikings sailed whole fleets up all the major rivers of Europe; among the cities they plundered were Paris, Aachen, Mainz, Trier and Cologne.

Thousands of miles to the south and east, fleets of Norse marauders terrorised the coasts of the Mediterranean, the Black Sea, even the Caspian. Viking traders reached Byzantium - the "Great City" on the coast of modern Turkey, which had inherited much of the power of ruined Rome - by way of the mighty rivers through Russia, often

(Far left) Apart from plundering the rest of Europe, Vikings regularly faced each other as enemies, on every scale from a raid on a neighbouring village to the several invasions of Norway by the Danes. Struggles for a crown, or attempts to impose or resist the new Christian religion, also led to fierce internal battles.

(Left) At the Carolingian and Norman courts of the early medieval period falconry was a common pastime, and we can assume that the Vikings knew it. Since most Scandinavians were more usually engaged in a daily struggle to survive, however, this hobby was probably not widespread before the more prosperous Norman settlements of the 10th and 11th centuries.

(Above) Besides the longship and the Danish axe, the round shield is the third well-known symbol of the Vikings - although it was used by nearly every European warrior in the early Middle Ages. This Viking might be on sentry duty at one of the countless camps that were set up by Scandinavian raiding parties during the years of their devastation of coastal Europe. In 860, for example, the Vikings coolly encamped on the island of Jeufosse close to Paris, knowing that the Frankish troops on the banks of the Seine could not reach them. Although on this occasion the Vikings did not carry on up river, they came back in 886 and besieged Paris.

dragging their ships over portages between one river and another. In time many Vikings enlisted to serve the Byzantine emperors as mercenaries, and this Varangian Guard gained an elite reputation throughout Europe and the Near East.

Viking settlement also resulted in the founding of the duchy of Normandy, when in 911 the West Frankish king gave land to a Viking army led by Rolf "the Ganger". The Franks later tried more than once to drive out the Norsemen, but they and their descendants quickly became too powerful to be brought to heel by the French throne. The Normans in their turn crossed the Channel to defeat the Anglo-Saxons in 1066, and their Duke William the Bastard won the title of King William I of England, "the Conqueror". But even this grim soldier-monarch was not immune to attack: in 1067 William, the descendant of a Viking who had taken land instead of *danegeld* (protection money), had to pay danegeld himself to King Svein Estridson of Denmark. This was, however, the last successful attempt to plunder England.

The Normans, one of the hardiest and most voracious peoples in European history, spread their baronies to many corners of the continent. The conversion of Scandinavia to Christianity diminished the activities of the Viking pirates, slave traders and raiders. Europe now looked east, to the Holy Land; and the years 1096-99 saw the First Crusade, with soldiers from Denmark, Norway and Sweden fighting under the banner of the Cross alongside those of other European nations.

(Left) Contrary to the popular image, we know today that only large warships displayed the legendary dragon-carved bow and stern posts. This smaller, plainer type of vessel, as reconstructed by the re-enactment society Regia Anglorum, probably represents a more typical appearance. The Bayeux Tapesty includes interesting scenes of the building of the ships for William of Normandy's invasion fleet in 1066 which parallel what archaeologists can deduce from Viking ship finds.

(Above) The wolfish appearance of this re-enactor convincingly suggests the fearsome reputation of the "Norsemen" throughout Europe in the early Middle Ages. The Scandinavian peoples referred to themselves simply as Swedes, Danes, Norwegians, etc.; *viking* described an activity - that of raiding abroad - rather than a group.

(**Above**) A common sight all over Europe during the early Middle Ages: the ships of a Scandinavian trading expedition have arrived up-river, and the crews prepare to land their cargo. Viking traders were no less enterprising than raiders - indeed, plunderers often targeted some new area on hearing tales of prosperity and weak defences from returning traders.

(**Right**) The Hollywood image (based on 19th century misinterpretations) of the wild Viking with his bearskin cloak and horned helmet leaping from his dragon-ship is now known to be inaccurate. Some of these clichés have slight roots in archaeological evidence, but most are completely false; the horned helmet, in particular, flies in the face of all evidence. This man, like many, is too poor to own a helmet. He wears a padded *gambeson* over his tunic, and is armed with a spear with crosspieces and a *fransisca* throwing axe, both of Frankish origin.

Chronology

789	First known Viking landing in England; official sent by Anglo-Saxon King Beorthric to question small landing party is killed.
792	Anglo-Saxon King Offa starts to organize the defence of Kent against Vikings.
793	Norwegian Vikings destroy island monastery of Lindisfarne off NE English coast in first recorded raid.
795	Vikings raid Rathlin island and Irish mainland monasteries.
799	Viking raids at the mouth of the Loire, France.
(800-900	Viking raids throughout century lead to destructionof all Anglo-Saxon kingdoms except Wessex.)
(c.806-865	Swedish Vikings under Rurik settle around Lake Ladoga, N Russia, and take over Novgorod.)
808	King Gottrik of Denmark destroys Slavic trading centre at Reric and moves traders to his nearby new foundation, Haithabu.
810	Danish Vikings attack Carolingian province of Friesia.
c.830	Norwegian Vikings, by now established in the islands off N Scotland, raid deep into Ireland.
(830-850	Continuous Viking raids on coasts of southern England and of France.)
834-837	Annual raids on Dorestad in Friesia.
835	King Egbert of Wessex defeats Danish Vikings, but other landings ravage Isle of Sheppey in Thames estuary.
840	Vikings spend winter in Ireland for first time.
841	Viking fort established on banks of the Liffey on site of modern Dublin; Vikings loot Rouen, France.
842-843	Vikings plunder Quentovic, France; sail up Loire, attack Nantes, and winter in France for first time.
844	Viking ships sail up the Garonne, France; and also take Seville, Spain, but driven out immediately by Moors.
845	120 Danish ships sail up Seine, attack Paris; Frankish King Charles the Bald buys their retreat for 7,000 pounds of silver - the first *danegeld* of 13 payments by 926. Hamburg, Germany, destroyed by Vikings.
850-851	Viking army winters in England for first time, at Thanet; defeated by King Ethelwulf of Wessex, which becomes heart of Anglo-Saxon resistance.
852	Swedish Vikings demand danegeld from citizens of Novgorod.
855/856	Vikings winter on Isle of Sheppey, Thames estuary.
857	Danes loot Paris.
858	Swedish Vikings found Kiev.
859-862	Viking fleet loots cities on Mediterranean coasts.
860	Vikings attack Byzantium without success.
c.860	Norwegian Vikings discover Iceland.
862	Cologne, Germany, looted by Vikings.
863	Viking raid on Xanten, Germany.
865	Danish "Great Army" lands in England in search of permanent conquest, and by 870 has conquered large areas in north and east - "the Danelaw".
866	Kent pays first danegeld.
866/867	Salomon, Duke of Brittany, defeats Franks at Brissarthe with aid of Viking mercenaries.
c.870	Harald Finehair unites Norway and becomes sole king; King Edmund of East Anglia defeated and killed by Danes.
870-930	Settlement of Iceland.
871	Danish Vikings defeated by Anglo-Saxons under Ethelred I and Alfred of Wessex at Ashdown.
c.872	Sea battle of Hafrsfjord between Harald Finehair and a union of north and west Norwegian leaders; Danes take Anglo-Saxon kingdom of Mercia.
878	After early setbacks, Alfred of Wessex defeats Danes under Guthrum at Edington.
881	Viking raids on Aachen, Worms, Metz, Bonn and Cologne.
882	Oleg the Wise unites Novgorod and Kiev. Viking raid on Trier.
884-885	Danish attacks in Kent repulsed by Alfred, who retakes London; Danes forced to accept Peace of Wedmore, fixing southern border of the Danelaw; Alfred the Great becomes king of Saxon England.
886	Paris besieged for 11 months by 40,000 Vikings, 700 ships.
887/888	Vikings paid to fight Burgundian rebels by Frankish King Charles the Fat.
891	Viking army defeated by East Franks in Belgium.
892-896	King Alfred defeats Danish "Great Army" from Europe and forces survivors to flee to Danelaw or France; Saxon successes against Viking ships in sea fights.
c.900	Danes and Orkadian Norwegians under Rolf

	the Ganger raid and later settle between the Loire and Seine, France.
902	Irish drive the Norwegians out of Dublin.
907	Oleg leads fleet down Dniepr to Black Sea, clashes with Byzantine forces.
910-912	Vikings sail the Caspian Sea as pirates.
911	Rolf the Ganger granted Normandy as fief of Frankish King Charles the Simple. Treaty between Byzantium and the Rus is the first written reference to Viking mercenaries in the Byzantine army - by 988 the number of these "Varangians" would increase to c.6,000.
912	Rolf of Normandy takes name Rollo on conversion to Christianity.
917-919	Norwegians recapture Dublin; Vikings from Ireland capture Danish centre of York.
924	Saxon King Edward the Elder reconquers much of the Danelaw after 20-year campaign.
934	German King Henry the Fowler defeats Danish King Chnuba at Haithabu.
c.937	Battle of Brunanburh - Olaf Guthfrithsson leads Vikings from Ireland and Norwegian parts of the Danelaw to defeat in two days' fighting against Saxons and Viking mercenaries under King Athelstan.
940-954	York remains temporarily an independent Viking kingdom.
c.950	King Haakon the Good tries to convert Norway to Christianity.
954	Eadred drives Eric Bloodaxe, last Viking king, out of York; England once again under Anglo-Saxon rule.
958	Harald Bluetooth becomes king of Denmark.
962-965	Harald Bluetooth re-establishes Danish control over Norway; embraces Christianity, and thereafter converts Denmark.
974	German Emperor Otto II captures the Danewerk, a fortification on the Frankish-Danish border. Harald Bluetooth reconquers these territories in 983.
(c.980-1014	Renewed Viking raids on England; King Ethelred II "the Ill-Advised" suffers repeated defeats despite massive danegeld payments; 991, he mounts atrocious massacre of English-born Danes.)
980	Battle of Tara - Irish-based Norwegians defeated by Irish, and thereafter have to pay tribute.
c.982-985	Eric the Red explores Greenland; in c.985, he leads colonising expedition of some

	25 ships. Bjarni Herjolfsson fails to make landfall in Greenland and reaches North America instead.
991	Battle of Maldon - Wessex troops under Ealdorman Byhrtnoth defeated by Viking army under Olaf Tryggvasson and Thorkell the Great.
995-1000	Olaf Tryggvasson reigns as king of Norway until defeated and killed in sea battle of Svoldr by Danes and Swedes.
c.1000	Following Bjarni Herjolfsson's tales, Leif Ericson and his brother Thorwals explore "Vinland" on NE American coast.
1013	Danish King Svein Forkbeard recognised by the Danelaw.
1014	Irish under King Brian Boru defeat Norwegian Vikings at decisive battle of Clontarf. Cnut the Great, son of Svein Forkbeard, defeats 'all the nobility of England' at battle of Ashingdon; 1016, establishes short-lived Anglo-Nordic kingdom.
1015/1016	Olaf Haraldsson (St.Olaf) wins throne of Norway.
1028	Olaf Haraldsson driven out of Norway, and killed 1030 at battle of Stiklastad.
1035-1043	After death of Cnut the Great, Hardacnut (1035-1042) becomes king of England & Denmark and Magnus the Good (1035-1047) king of Norway. 1042, Magnus reunites Denmark and Norway; 1043, defeats Slavs at Haithabu.
(1047-1066	Harald Sigurdsson "Hardrada" reigns as king of Norway;
1047-1074	Svein Estridson reigns as king of Denmark.)
1050	Harald Hardrada destroys Haithabu.
1066	Harald Hardrada invades N England; defeated and killed by Saxon King Harold Godwinsson at Stamford Bridge, 25 September. William of Normandy leads simultaneous Norman invasion of S England; Saxon army force-marches south, but King Harold is defeated and killed at Hastings, 14 October.
1067	Svein Estridson raids England, William the Conqueror pays danegeld.
1079	Icelander Godred Corvan raids Isle of Man, then subject to Dublin Vikings, and establishes Norwegian rule.
1085	Final Viking raid on England by Danish King Cnut fails.

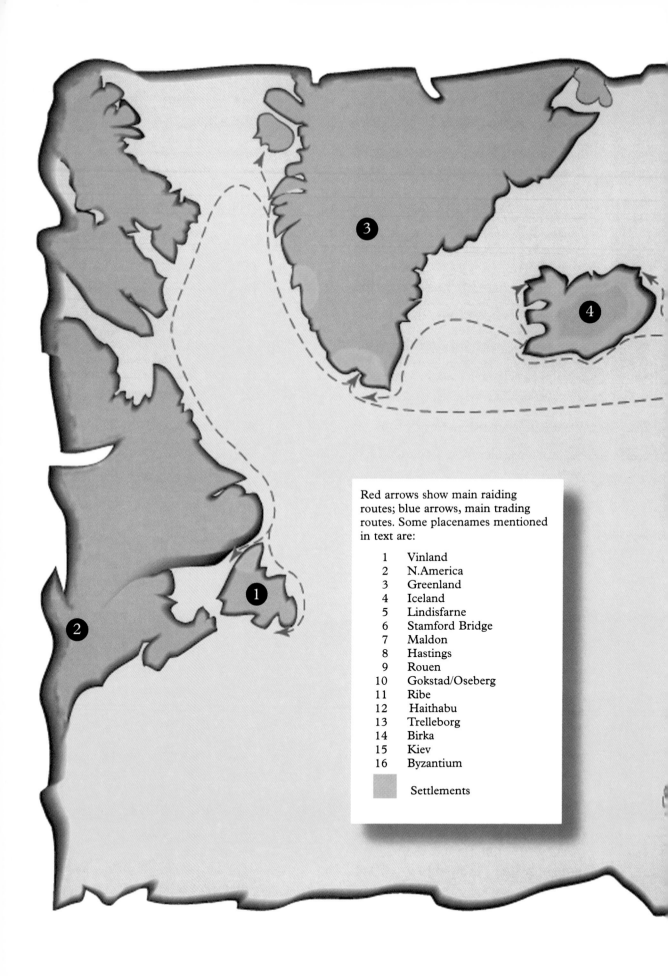

Red arrows show main raiding
routes; blue arrows, main trading
routes. Some placenames mentioned
in text are:

1   Vinland
2   N.America
3   Greenland
4   Iceland
5   Lindisfarne
6   Stamford Bridge
7   Maldon
8   Hastings
9   Rouen
10 Gokstad/Oseberg
11 Ribe
12 Haithabu
13 Trelleborg
14 Birka
15 Kiev
16 Byzantium

    Settlements

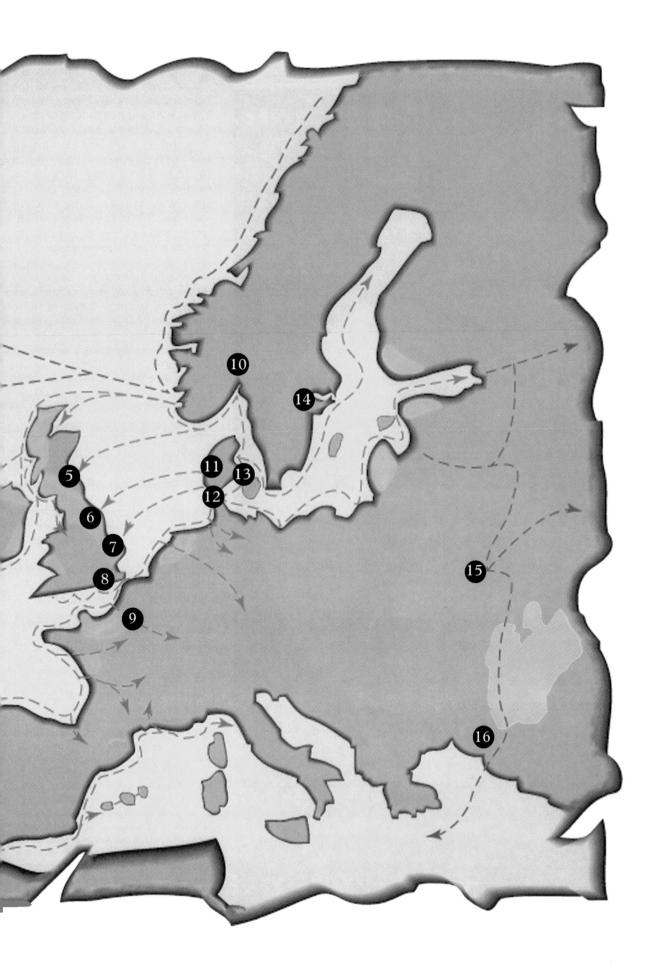

The Common Warrior

Only a minority of the Viking warriors who formed the early raiding parties or the later armies were wealthy enough to have expensive weapons or armour. The bulk of these forces consisted of so-called *karls*, probably armed only with a spear or axe and a shield. These were free men, perhaps owning a little farming land, who had the right to carry weapons. These men would volunteer to joining a plundering expedition mounted by a wealthier local *hersir* or a noble *jarl* or, later, a major undertaking led by a king; there were also karls who were bound by various kinds of allegiance to a hersir. To these peasants, originally very poor, a successful raiding party could mean real wealth; after deducting a major share for the shipowner and perhaps others for some privileged members of the party, any loot was divided equally among the crew.

The individual was responsible for providing his own equipment, and this would rarely have included anything that was not available on his own farm. Archaeologists assume that every warrior going on an expedition carried his personal belongings in a wooden chest, which served him as a rowing bench aboard ship. While he was away his wife would run the farm in his stead, with any dependent male relatives and slaves to do the daily work and defend the land and stock.

(Left) Most Vikings would only have been armed with weapons available in their households, such as an axe or a *sax* (a heavy, single-edged knife). The surprise and ferocity of their raids often made up for any individual lack of equipment, however. To protect himself this warrior carries a round wooden shield, made of thin planks bound with leather at the rim - metal binding and fittings have also been found. A central iron boss covers the hole which accomodates the fist where it holds the handgrip fixed across the rear. Finds show that shields were often made from limewood, and some are only about 6mm (0.2in.) thick for lightness. Size varied between about 60cm and 100cm (24ins-40ins), but the shield would always cover the torso.

(Right) The sax is a weapon which seems to have been typical for Vikings of the English Danelaw and Ireland, who presumably adopted it from the Saxons; few saxes have been found among burial goods in Scandinavia itself, where the axe was the everyday weapon and tool. The hilt of the sax pictured here is made of horn, and shows an unusual brass cross-guard - our common warrior has probably looted it in England or Ireland.

(Left) An undyed tunic and trousers are the complete summer clothing for this Viking, though he will have owned a thick, warm woollen tunic or a woollen cloak for the winter. His axe is decorated with carving. Around his neck he wears a comb and some good luck charms on a leather thong; but he does not display any jewellery, and the clasp with which he closes his tunic is of simple quality.

(Right) Normally a poor warrior would not own shoes, but our subject wears a pair made of goatskin in a form following archaeological finds at Norwich, East Anglia - a so-called "turnshoe", closed at the outside with two leather toggles. Knee-high leg wrappings protect him from cold, mud and thorns.

Edged Weapons

The devastating victories which the Vikings won all over Europe seem out of proportion with their rather simple arsenal - it is not to any significant superiority in weapons that we should look for the secrets of their success. The warrior's equipment was virtually the same right across Europe in the 7th-11th centuries, and between any two regions weapons usually differed only in details of design and quality (though some areas seem to show evidence of a traditional attachment to one weapon or another). Viking weapons were fairly simple, and except for the sword most could also be used in everyday life at home - an axe for cutting wood, spears and bows for hunting, and a single-edged knife for a multitude of household tasks. Only the sword was developed solely as a lethal weapon.

Spears

Though historians and archaeologists still dispute the question of the predominant weapon of the early Middle Ages, it is very likely to have been the spear. Spearheads needed only relatively little iron, were cheap and easy to forge, and could be supplied in great numbers; every owner could shaft his own. The finds of spearheads in nearly every warrior's grave indicate that they were common. They had many uses, and we should distinguish between different types.

Light spears or javelins were thrown. The warrior usually carried several of them as a distance weapon. The account of the battle of Maldon in 991 tells of a Viking injured by an Anglo-Saxon javelin piercing his ringmail shirt; this makes the point that the impact of a spear thrown by a trained warrior could force open the rings of riveted mail.

The impact of thrusts delivered with hand-held spears must have been even greater. Controlled single- or two-handed, they could not only be used to thrust with the point but also to cut with the edges of the spearhead, to deliver blows with the shaft, and to block enemy blows. The so-called "winged" spearheads, thought to have been a Carolingian invention, feature two sideways projections from the socket of the spearhead; these could be used to hook behind shield rims and pull the shield away, but also to hook the body of the opponent. (The reason for the original design was probably that the projections also prevented the spearhead penetrating so deeply into the body of an animal or a foe that it was difficult to pull out.)

Spear shafts varied in length between about 150cm and 300cm (5ft-10ft), with 20cm-60cm (8in-24in) heads. The shaft was usually made from ash and had a diameter of about 2.5cm (one inch). The socketed heads came in a wide variety of shapes: long and narrow, short, leaf-bladed, flat, round, or with a triangular cross-section. Many recovered examples are made from pattern-welded iron, often decorated with silver wire inlays; but as most finds are from rich

(Left) Numerous spearheads of different shapes and sizes have been found in graves and on battlefield or settlement sites. Scandinavian spearheads are usually long and narrow, like the two right hand examples here - although the projecting "wings" are of Carolingian origin. The spear second from left shows another typical form, of Celtic origin but imported to Scandinavia. The shapes of spearheads stayed nearly unchanged throughout the whole Viking period.

(Right) This group of warriors carry not only spears but also a number of shorter, lightweight javelins. Early medieval paintings and tapestries show warriors carrying three or four javelins; as soon as they were thrown the warrior would continue fighting with his sword or axe, which he carried at his belt. Sometimes warriors are depicted carrying the javelins in the same hand as the shield. Although the basic spear was a relatively cheap weapon it was by no means carried only by poor men - the jarl or hersir was as likely to carry a finely decorated example.

(Left) This battlefield picture, taken during a re-enactment show at Trelleborg, Sweden, shows the proportions of the weapons used: a high number of axes and spears, but only two of the expensive swords. The deformation of the shield (left) shows the momentum of a spear thrust. Whether they were used one- or two-handed, spears were capable of piercing both shields and mail. The front line of a battle array was composed of warriors with axe or sword and shield, and the spearmen would thrust over their heads, trying to stay behind the "shield wall".

warriors' graves, this does not necessarily mean that spearheads were normally decorated. When held single-handed the spear was most likely wielded overarm for a downwards thrust; this allowed stabs to the head and body, and from this position it could also be thrown without changing grip.

Axes

At the beginning of the Viking era both the normal woodcutter's axe and the small "bearded" axe were commonly used. Axes would be kept as tools in every Nordic household, so they would be available to even the poorest free-born warrior; but they soon developed into a symbol of the terror the Vikings spread among their enemies. They had 60cm-90cm (2ft-3ft) hafts and cutting edges 7cm-15cm (3ins-6ins) long. The *fransisca*, a small throwing axe probably developed by the Franks, was also used by Anglo-Saxons and Vikings alike.

The later years saw the invention of the notorious so-called "Danish axe" - long or broad axe - specifically a battle weapon, perhaps developed in response to the more widespread use of ringmail armour. On a 120cm-180cm (4ft-6ft) haft was mounted a large, heavy blade with a crescent-shaped edge about 22cm-45cm (9ins-18ins) long. Swung by a strong man, it could easily bring down a rider or smash

(**Above left**) The "Danish axe" became closely associated with the Vikings all over Europe – even in far-off Byzantium, where the Varangian Guard was referred to as the "guard of axe-bearers". This warrior additionally carries a sword from a belt over his right shoulder; his superior armour consists of a *spangenhelm* helmet and a mail shirt over his woollen tunic.

(**Left**) Examples of axeheads, including the great "Danish axe" (centre) - more properly called a *breidox*, broad axe. The symmetrically shaped axes (centre & bottom right) show thicker, harder steel edges welded to blades made from milder steel. The other four are examples of "bearded axe" - s*keggox* - with different types of "beards". Note projections of the socket to give a better fit and prevent breaking of the haft. It was the Vikings who introduced the axe to northern Europe as a popular weapon.

(**Right**) Surprised while looting a longhouse, Vikings defend themselves. The warrior wearing helmet and padded gambeson tries ward off his enemy's sword with his axe; in the background his comrade is getting into trouble, as his opponent has thrust his axe through the shield and will now try to pull it away. This picture reminds us that the axe was not only good for delivering blows but also for hooking and pulling, and the tips of its blade for thrusting.

shields. It also allowed thrusts with the axehead and, like the winged spearhead, it could be hooked behind a shield and pulled to break an opposing "shield wall".

Saxes

The sax was another item in everyday use which was also suitable as a weapon, and was probably carried by warriors of all ranks. The Coppergate excavations in York turned up 300 saxes; and though this was an Anglo-Saxon find, York was long a Viking centre. As indicated by the name, the origin of the sax lies with the Saxons, and the Vikings most probably adopted it from these peoples who were as often their neighbours as their enemies.

The sax is a single-edged knife of a length which can range from about 7.5cm to 75cm (3-30 inches). We can distinguish between two groups: short ones with a length of 35cm (14ins) or less, and long ones of between 50cm and 75cm (20-30 inches). Originally the shorter knives were probably everyday domestic tools, carried to war for camp use but also ready to hand if a fallen enemy had to be finished off. The long saxes were developed specifically as weapons, but they could equally be used for more peaceful chores, in the manner of a machete. Some long saxes fitted with sword-type handles were found in the Irish Viking burials of Kilmainham-Islandbridge.

Sax blades were straight and single-edged, the back of the blade often broad and the blade thus quite heavy; it was tapered to the tip, which was sharpened to allow thrusting. The rare Scandinavian finds feature a slightly downwards-turned edge. The sax

was carried in a scabbard of folded leather, which might be decorated with copper, bronze or silver if the wealth of the owner allowed. As with spearheads, axes and swords, some finds show silver inlayed decoration.

Swords

The sword was the most expensive weapon a warrior might carry, and hilts and crossguards were often highly decorated with patterned copper or silver and niello inlays to show off the rank and wealth of the owner. The sword was not merely a practical tool, but in this warrior culture was sometimes believed to have mystic properties - individual swords were named, and skilled smiths were believed to have access to magic powers. In the small part of the town of Haithabu which has been excavated to date the remains of 40 swords of all qualities have already been found.

The Viking sword had a double-edged blade about 72cm-82cm (28ins-32ins) long and perhaps 5cm (2ins) wide. The hilt added another 7.5cm-10cm (3ins-4ins), giving an overall length of just under one meter, which seems to have increased towards the end of the Viking era. A short crossguard protected the hand; and at the end of the hilt a heavy pommel acted as a balancing counterweight for the blade, without which the sword - weighing up to 2kg (4.5lbs) - would have been difficult to control.

At the beginning of the Viking age pattern-welded blades were thought to be the best: this was the complex technique of welding and forging together rods of pure iron and of carbonised iron, i.e. steel.

(Left) Reconstructions of various saxes found in England, Ireland and (lower three) Scandinavia - the latter showing the very slightly down-curved blade shape. The example (second left) with a crossguard is not long enough to be called a sword-sax. Hilts were made from wood, horn or bone, and although some of the saxes pictured here have a two-piece riveted grip other finds have the tang running up into a pierced single-piece hilt.

The result is a hard but nevertheless flexible blade which shows a beautiful surface pattern after it is polished. Some blade finds have a pattern-welded core combined with harder steel edges. One 10th century English reference puts the cost of a sword of superb quality at 15 male slaves or 120 oxen.

In the 9th century the European sword market was taken over by Frankish smiths (although King Charles the Bald tried to ban the export of these "strategic weapons" from his territories). The Franks had discovered that they could achieve better results by using phosphorised steel; this did require specialist knowledge in forging, but was quicker than pattern-welding. The Scandinavian smiths, who had not yet mastered this new technique, imported unfinished blades from the Franks and completed and hilted them to the Viking taste. Blades of Frankish origin have been found in Denmark, Norway, Sweden, the Baltic states, England and Ireland.

The scabbards were made from wood covered with leather and were usually lined with oiled material to protect the sword from rusting; they usually had a metal chape to protect the tip, and sometimes metal reinforcement at the mouth. They were initially slung from a belt which ran over the shoulder, held in place by the waist belt; later in our period they were often hung directly from the waist belt.

Vikings swords were used single-handed, combined with a shield or sax in the other hand. When delivering a blow care had to be taken not to strike directly onto the opponent's sword, as the steel - high quality by the standards of their age, but rather brittle by ours - would break easily.

(Above right) The long-hafted "Danish axe" with its crescentic blade became widespread at the end of the 10th century. The cutting surface, which was between 9ins and 12ins long (there is one reference to an 18in example), often had a welded edge of higher quality steel. Like Viking swords, axes were sometimes named; female names were apparently favoured, and King Olaf Haraldsson had one named *Hel* after the Norse goddess of death. In the hands of a tall, strong man the long axe was a devastating weapon, and there are many tales of the dreadful damage it could do, to armoured men and their horses alike.

(Right) This warrior is armed with sword and shield but also carries an axe in his belt. The Arabian chronicler Ibn Miskawayh described Scandinavian warriors raiding a trading post in 943; each carried a sword, but fought with shield and spear, and also had an axe and/or knife in his belt. Note the short ringmail shirt of the early Viking age, with its "dagged" lower edge, and the mail neckguard on the helmet.

(Above) The warrior in front of this line is equipped with helmet, ringmail, sword and shield; his equipment is similar to that found in a Viking burial at Gjermundbu, Norway, presumably the grave of a wealthy 10th century leader. The grave also contained a bridle.

(Left) Details of two reconstructed sword hilts, showing the complex decoration of pommels and crossguards. The left hand example is similar to a Jutland find; the original was inlaid with silver and brass. The right hand sword was copied from a find in southern Sweden, although the original piece was made in England in around 1000 AD; the crossguard and pommel mounting were made from silver, gilded and decorated with niello (the pommel was missing from the original and was speculatively reconstructed). To the right the fittings of a scabbard can be seen, also richly decorated.

(Above) These three reconstructed sword hilts show some of the many common variants. The two to the left are silver plated like the splendid Haithabu sword find; note two-piece wooden grips. The right hand example features a five-lobed pommel, with silver inlay and silver wire. This shape of hilt is similar to one found in the ship-burial at Haithabu and dated to the middle of the 9th century, though the original is much more highly decorated. (Left & right photos courtesy Dawn of Time Crafts)

(Right) Although many highly decorated grave finds seem to tell a different story, the typical Viking sword is assumed to have been fairly plain - few warriors could afford craftsmanship in precious metals, and the owner would judge the value of a sword by the quality of the blade, not the amount of decoration.

The Viking Hersir

(Left) The fact that he owns helmet, sword and ringmail corselet shows the considerable wealth of this warrior - the latter, particularly, has seldom been found in Scandinavian burials. His mail reaches the thigh and has short sleeves, which suggests a relatively early date. It is fastened at the upper back by leather lacing sewn to the rings. Note also the detail of the mail's construction: each ring is linked with four others. In today's reconstructed mail, for the sake of time and expense, the rings are not riveted or forged closed but only butted over; there are also period examples of this method among the archaeological record.

(Right) The "dagged" lower edge of the ringmail shirt; this effect did not serve any practical purpose but was purely decorative. (There is clear evidence for its use nearly a thousand years before by Roman auxiliary troops.) Under his mail and over his woollen tunic our hersir wears a quilted leather jerkin or *gambeson* stuffed with hair, wool or even hay.

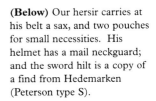

(Left) Leather boots like these were fastened with toggles made from wood or horn. Some additional strips of leather are fitted to the leather sole to give a sort of cleating for a better grip. The basic model for this boot is a leather "turnshoe", of which examples have been found at many sites; a high leg could be added to give better protection in winter.

(Below) Our hersir carries at his belt a sax, and two pouches for small necessities. His helmet has a mail neckguard; and the sword hilt is a copy of a find from Hedemarken (Peterson type S).

This warrior could be a *hersir*, a term identifying a wealthy farmer owning his own land and having the status of a local leader or chief of a clan. At the beginning of the Viking age the hersirs were the organisers and leaders of raiding parties and settlements, but their influence decreased with the late 10th century, when effective national monarchies evolved in Scandinavia. Thereafter the hersir became a local representative of royal power.

The beliefs of our hersir seem to be at the border between paganism and Christianity; he wears a combined symbol of the cross and Thor's hammer around his neck, decorated with a wolf's head - this amulet originated in Iceland and is dated to the 10th century, when Iceland converted to Christianity. The painting on his shield pictures a scene described in the *Prose Edda* by Snorri Sturlusson: two wolves chase the sun and moon across the skies, and thus cause alternating day and night. If the wolves should one day catch their quarry they will devour them, and *Ragnarok* will come - the end of the world, according to the Nordic pagan religion. Then the fallen heroes will leave Valhalla to ride to their last battle at the side of the gods of Asgard, fighting against the giants; and the death of the gods will bring the world we know to an end.

Perhaps our hersir has even been baptised, though this did not necessarily mean much to a Viking. Sometimes they would receive baptism to improve trade with the Christian peoples; sometimes they would accept it only for the sake of the presents handed out to new believers; sometimes the new faith was embraced in prudent obedience to a king. Even if the convert attended church while on dry land, he often continued to sacrifice to his old gods when sailing the seas.

23

Armour and Helmets

Those among the Vikings and their enemies who could afford to do so wore several different types of armour. This was a highly desirable possession, since the wounds of edged weapons could quickly prove deadly in an unhygienic age ignorant of medicine. A cut just a centimetre deep could easily lead to tetanus or blood poisoning, and penetration wounds which carried dirty clothing or other debris into the body were lethally vulnerable to infection.

Some readers may assume that the **ringmail shirt** (*brynja* or *hringserkr*) was the typical Viking armour. As already stated, its cost in fact made it a rarity in the 8th-10th centuries, but it was certainly used to some extent. Contemporary depictions and the rare archaeological finds confirm that at the beginning of the Viking age in the 8th century mail reached to the crotch and had short sleeves - e.g. the Gjermundbu find from Norway, in which 85 fragments of a 9th-century corselet were discovered.

During the 11th century - when the equipment of the fighting men of most northern European peoples became more similar - mail shirts grew longer. The Bayeux Tapestry shows Norman and Anglo-Saxon warriors of 1066 with mostly a knee-length mail coat or *hauberk*, divided at both front and back from the lower edge to the crotch to allow it to be worn on horseback. In this final period of the Viking age additional pieces were also added to the original, simple T-shaped mail corselet: coifs or mail hoods covered the head, and ventails - rectangular flaps - were fastened across the face with laces or hooks to protect the area not covered by a helmet.

Depending on the size of the rings - which were probably never the same from any two blacksmiths - and on the length of the corselet, a single mail shirt could contain anything from 20,000 to 60,000 rings. The rings can be separated into two types: some were punched like flat washers from a metal plate, and others were made from drawn wire. The wire rings also appear in two varieties - closed and open.

To construct a mail shirt, four of the closed rings were hooked into one open one, which was then riveted. These groups of five rings could then be brought together with another open ring, assembly continuing in all directions. The weight of an 11th century knee-length, long-sleeved ringmail hauberk was approximately 18kg (40lbs), and it could take a whole year to make. This explains why only wealthy warriors could afford to buy one - we may guess that the price might be comparable to that of a luxury car today.

It is difficult to say how rare they really were, however. Mail seems seldom to have been buried

(**Above**) This warrior's ringmail shirt is of the 8th century T-shaped type; the lower edge reaches the thigh and is dagged for decoration. Some kind of protective clothing like his padded gambeson must normally have been worn below the mail to spread the impact of blows. To make it easier for the warrior to move his arms this mail shirt has been left open at the armpits - a trade-off between flexibility and protection.

with its owners; if properly protected from rust and skillfully repaired when necessary it would last almost indefinitely, and most likely these valuable items were handed down over the generations. They were far too precious to be simply lost, or to be left on the battlefield in an age when plundering the dead was commonplace. In the later medieval period, when we know mail to have been common, battlefield grave finds are still most unusual, and more formal Christian burials no longer included "grave goods".

Below ringmail the warrior would wear a **gambeson**, a tunic- like piece of clothing made from two layers of wool, leather or linen stuffed with an interlining of fleece, animal hair or some similar material. The layers were then sewn together by quilting. Its purpose was to spread the impact of blows, to prevent crush injuries and to stop broken ringmail from being forced into the flesh. If it was made from leather it was in itself a good protection against cuts, and was often worn instead of mail.

Another type of armour which should be mentioned

is **lamellar**, which was uncommon in western Europe and had its roots in the Middle East. But as the Vikings reached Byzantium on their raiding and trading voyages, and are even thought to have visited Baghdad, they are likely to have known this type of armour. Lamellar consists of small steel scales - lamellae - with holes punched through at the edges, allowing them to be overlapped and laced together into corselets. Lamellae of different shapes and sizes have been found at the site of Birka, a trading city in central Sweden. Although tests show that these were trade goods and had not been made up into armours, what would be the sense in importing them over a long distance if there were no use for them?

A final type of protection which may have been used were vambraces (arm pieces) and greaves made from steel **splints**, about 16mm (^{5}/8in) wide and of varying length, mounted on leather strapping and worn on the lower legs and/or arms. The ancestors of the

Vikings are also thought to have had a similar type of body armour, as suggested by interpretation of the c.6th-7th century Välsgarde find in Uppland, Sweden.

Helmets

There is only one well-preserved find of a helmet that is undoubtedly of Viking origin - that found at Gjermundbu, dated to the late 9th century. The helmet consists of a brow band to which two curved strips are fixed to make a dome, one running from the front to the back and the other from ear to ear; at their junction is a small spike. The strips form a frame for four concave triangular plates which fill in the skull of the helmet. The face is partially covered by a "visor" shaped like the frame of spectacles or goggles, decorated with inlaid eyebrows; and a mail neckguard was originally attached to the back and

(Right) Over his mail this warrior wears lamellar armour protecting his upper body. In the eastern countries where this type of armour originated lamellae have been found variously shaped at the lower edges, including shield shapes. (The contemporary Slavs also had helmets of laced lamellar construction). Our warrior's helmet is beaten from a single piece of steel but has a riveted-on nasal bar not unlike the Olmütz helmet find. Beneath it a leather-lined mail coif is visible; these became common in the 11th century. Note the different mail ring sizes and wire thicknesses - there is plentiful archaeological evidence for this.

(**Left**) Those who could not afford mail might wear a padded gambeson alone, in shapes similar to those of mail corselets. Gambesons depicted on stones, tapestries and wooden figurines show the lines of stitched quilting in both square-set and diagonal patterns; this example of the former is reconstructed using woollen fabric.

(**Below**) This gambeson is diagonally quilted, and split at the sides so that despite its knee length it will not hamper movement when fighting. If thick enough, padded leather gambesons gave some protection from cuts; there is an early 11th century reference to reindeer hide gambesons from Lapland giving comparable protection to mail.

sides. All parts of the helmet were riveted together.

Although this is a unique survival, documented finds of visor pieces at a number of other Scandinavian sites confirm its widespread use. It appears to be a simplified development of a much more elaborate helmet construction of the Vendel age, 100-200 years previously. A number of these lavishly decorated pre-Viking age helmets were found at Välsgarde, also showing both spectacle-shaped visors and attached ringmail; these were made from many small decorated metal plates held together by metal bands forming a hemisphere.

From about 900 use of another type of helmet became widespread throughout Europe: the *spangenhelm*, not unlike the Gjermundbu helmet but with a more pointed dome, a straight nasal bar in front to protect the face, and in-fill plates of steel, hardened leather, or even horn. Runestone carvings show that this type of helmet was worn by many Vikings.

Following not long after the spangenhelm came the development of a similar conical helmet beaten from a single piece of steel; good examples are the Olmütz find and the "Wenceslas" helmet now in Prague. Both have a nasal bar, although the Wenceslas helmet has its richly decorated, cross-shaped nasal riveted to the skull rather than drawn down from it in one piece. Apart from the helmet types described a multitude of varieties and combinations may be imagined. One find features only the four triangular

The making of ringmail was very time-consuming, but required few tools, and could be undertaken in virtually any smithy. The making of the rings started with drawing the wire from hot or cold iron. The wire was then wound around a rod former in a coil, and separated into single rings with chisel cuts. A proportion of these rings were then forced through a cone so that the ends of the wire met; heated glowing red in the fire, these could be forged closed with a few hammer blows on the anvil. Other rings had the ends hammered flat and over-lapping, a hole being punched through these so that they could later be riveted.

plates, riveted directly together without any frame.

The interior of the helmets cannot be reconstructed exactly from archaeological evidence, but it is likely that a leather band or lining piece was riveted to the inside to which a chin strap or thongs were attached. Many warriors would also have worn padded caps to give a comfortable fit and extra protection against blows. Although a helmet was a lot cheaper than a mail corselet it is likely that only the richer sort owned one during the earlier period. Others had to protect their heads with caps of thick leather or fur, which are often pictured on runestones.

Pre-Viking age helmets had been richly decorated, but with the helmet becoming more common in 11th century Europe decoration appears less often; even those belonging to the wealthy usually had incised decoration only on the skull straps, brow bands, "eyebrows" or spectacles, and nasals. (There is reference, however, to the painting of "war marks" - *herkumbl* - on helmets, presumably some form of identifying sign.)

Finally, but importantly, we should emphasise that - Hollywood notwithstanding - Vikings did not wear horns on their helmets. This common error results partly from mistaken dating by early antiquaries of finds from other northern European cultures; and partly from various crude depictions of warrior figures who are dedicated to Odin. This is usually marked by a raven - Odin's bird - on the helmet, with the wings forming a circle to the left and right sides; often decorated, these can easily be mistaken for horns, especially as the raven's head often cannot be distinguished in profile.

(Below) This re-enactor wears mail of the early T-shape with a straight lower edge, and is armed with a "sword-sax". Fragments of a similar corselet were found together with the Gjermundbu helmet; ring diameter was about .85cm, about four rings per square centimetre (c.24 per square inch). Note that the arms were not made separately and fitted to the torso, but were fashioned as part of a single assembly.

(Opposite) This re-enactor wears a mail coif under his reconstruction of the "St. Wenceslas helmet" found in Prague. It was hammered from a single piece, with a cross-shaped nasal riveted to the front, and is dated to the 10th century. The decoration on the nasal suggests that the helmet originates in a Nordic culture.

(Above) This reconstruction shows the only relatively well-preserved helmet of unquestion-ably Viking origin and date - that found at Gjermundbu. It features a mail neckguard, a "spectacle- shaped" visor protecting eyes and nose, and a small spike at the junction of the two bands forming the skull frame. These, the brow band and the in-filling plates are riveted. The helmet probably belonged to a Viking leader who was buried in the 10th century together with his armour and sword. (Photo courtesy Dawn of Time Crafts)

(Right) The original of this "Vendel age" helmet was found at Välsgarde in Sweden. It cannot be dated with confidence, but was buried with its owner approximately 100-200 years before the Viking age, i.e. c.6th-7th centuries. Certain similarities to the 10th century Gjermundbu helmet are obvious - note the mail neckguard, and "spectacle" visor, here with bronze "eyebrows". This piece is richer in decoration and of more complex construction than the later type: embossed plates are fitted into edge pieces which are riveted to a frame. The plates show warrior figures carrying shield and spear and wearing coats and tunics, and helmets with "horns" - but these latter are probably meant to depict the wings of Odin's ravens, Hugin and Munin. The mail face- and neckguard is hooked onto a wire running through loops at the edge of the helmet; the maker of the Gjermundbu helmet punched holes into the edge for this purpose. (Photo courtesy Dawn of Time Crafts)

(**Below**) This picture shows a range of helmet types worn in Europe throughout the Viking age. (Left) is reconstructed after the Wenceslas helmet, but is not as richly decorated as the original. (Centre) is of spangenhelm construction with "eyebrows" and mail neckguard, as probably worn by the Vikings. (Right) is a reconstruction of the Gjermundbu helmet. Leather or fabric liners and chin laces are believed to have been fixed inside virtually all ancient and medieval helmets to enable them to be fitted securely to the head; some form of padding (e.g. sheepskin or quilted fabric?) would have been necessary for comfort and to protect against "blunt trauma".

(Above left) The so-called Giecz helmet is dated to the 11th century, and features four concave triangular plates riveted directly to one another; they are held together at the top by a plate with a plume-holder and at the bottom by a brow band. It is probably of Slavic origin; and like so many Viking age helmets, it has a mail neckguard fitted. Helmets of this construction may well have been worn by eastern Vikings such as the Rus, and could have reached Scandinavia as trade goods from these settlements - thus its use here in conjunction with an eastern lamellar corselet. (Photo courtesy Melanie Donus)

(Above right) Many Viking age warriors will have worn this combination of gambeson and spangenhelm. During the 11th century this type of helmet was the most common in Europe. Runestones show warriors wearing conical headgear which could be either spangenhelms, single-piece helmets similar to the "Wenceslas", or even simple leather caps.

(Left) This reconstructed spangenhelm has "eyebrows" above the nasal, clearly indi-cating Scandinavian manufac-ture. Although no complete helmet of this kind has been found, "eyebrows" associated with other helmet fragments have been recovered from many Viking burials, supporting this assumption. Note the leather edging to which the helmet liner is fitted; it is sewn through holes in the brow band, which could also have held a mail neckguard. Note also the long nasal, giving some protection against cuts to the face from the mouth up.

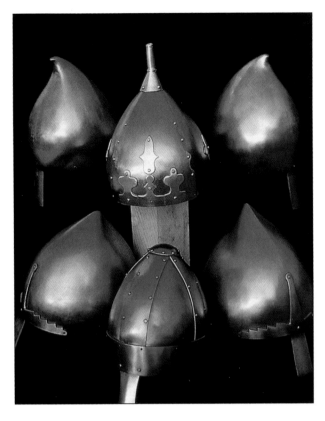

(Above) The helmet types reconstructed here are not originally Scandinavian, but some could very well have been imported, given the Vikings' wide-ranging operations. (Upper left & right) are of Norman make, similar to the Olmütz helmet except that the point of the skull is inclined to the front; while the Olmütz helmet is dated to the 11th century this type was found in the 12th century.

(Centre) is a front view of a Slavic helmet as perhaps worn by the Rus and Varangians; at the apex is a tubular holder for a horsehair plume. (Lower left & right) are two more reconstructions of the Wenceslas helmet. (Lower centre) is a spangenhelm, clearly showing the top plate covering the junction of the skull bands. (Photo courtesy Dawn of Time Crafts)

(Above right) Apart from the typically Scandinavian details like "eyebrows" and "spectacles", this replica of a pre-Viking age helmet has cheekguards to protect the face. These are a feature of several Vendel age helmets, and also of English finds of early Anglo-Saxon helmets, e.g. the Sutton Hoo and York

Coppergate examples. We can assume that they were still to be seen in the 8th and 9th centuries, as well as the metal strip neckguards also shown here; a combination of cheekguards and mail neck-guard, as on the Coppergate helmet, would also have been current. (Photo courtesy Dawn of Time Crafts)

(Right) This shows a span-genhelm with nasal to which cheekguards and a mail neck-guard have been fitted; cheek-guards might be attached either by rings or hinges.

Note also the large clasp with which our warrior fastens his cloak, of a Viking pattern dated to the 8th or 9th century.

The Varangian Guard

The Vikings fought not only as freelance plunderers and as the retainers of kings or local leaders, but also as paid mercenaries. A well-known example of this was the famous Varangian Guard of Byzantium. Although Scandinavian mercenaries are recorded in Byzantium earlier, the Guard itself was raised in 988 by the Emperor Basil II, who received 6,000 warriors from Vladimir of Kiev. The quality of Scandinavian fighting men was already well known in southern Europe. Earlier sources tell of 400 men taking part in a Byzantine expedition to Italy in 935; of at least 600 fighting with Byzantine troops on Crete in 949, and of others serving in 955 against the Arabs in the battle of Hadath.

From 988 the Varangian Guard formed a hard core unit of the Byzantine army, protecting the emperor, to whom they swore allegiance. This may be the origin of the term Varangian, perhaps coming from the word *var* meaning a group of men who had sworn allegiance. In Byzantium the Varangian Guard were known as the "axe-bearing barbarians" or the "guard of axe-bearers". Even today the names of

(Left) In Byzantium the members of the Varangian Guard were famous as men with red hair and beards, "as tall as date palms"; they were also said to drink too much. But the main symbol of the Varangians was the long-hafted Danish axe with its crescent-shaped edge. This guardsman wears ringmail, a mail coif and splint limb armour, and apart from his axe is armed with a sword and a knife.

(Right) In battle the Varangian protected his head with a mail coif and helmet. This spangenhelm has a very large decorated nasal with "eyebrows" and is obviously of northern origin, but similar helmets of Byzantine make would also have been widely worn. Pictorial sources also show ringmail worn under a smaller corselet of scale or lamellar armour. Note the fixing of the swordbelt passing over the right shoulder, as the Varangians usually wore it. Apart from Scandinavian swords they also used single-edged weapons from Byzantine armouries.

many Scandinavians who served in the guard survive. In the 11th century Byzantine troops in Greece were led by a guardsman named Ragnvald; and from 1035 to 1044 Harald Hardrada, who later became king of Norway, served in the guard and commanded 500 men.

The guardsmen were extremely well paid, and the income of Harald Hardrada is said to have given him the greatest personal fortune ever owned by a northern European at that date. On campaign the Varangian Guard also had the privilege of being the first to plunder a conquered city. It is also said that they were allowed to perform a ritual "raid" on the emperor's chambers at his accession (though there are other references to drunken guardsmen making serious attacks on Michael VII and on another emperor).

The clothing of the Varangians was of northern style but influenced by Slavic and Byzantine fashions. Contemporary sources often emphasise the Varangians' great two-handed axes, their Scandinavian drinking habits, their toughness and their height. They are said to have provided their own swords, but the bulk of their equipment would have been issued from Byzantine armouries. The guardsmen were usually heavily armoured, wearing both ringmail and lamellar armours.

(Above) Because of the weight, the mail corselets of the Byzantine army were usually relatively short with elbow-length sleeves. They were therefore combined with steel vambraces and greaves, by both Byzantine troops and the Varangians. The greaves illustrated are made from steel strips or "splints"; they are bent at the top and bottom to allow easier movement, and for a better fit the maker has used two different widths of strip.

(Left) The vambraces are of the same splint construction as the greaves; note strips of different length, the longer ones running up the outside. The sword belt supports the leather- covered wooden scabbard on the left hip, with the waist belt passing over it to keep it steady. The small leather pouch to the right of the scabbard might typically contain a pair of scissors to cut the beard and hair; a knife also hangs from the belt.

(**Right**) The rear view of our Varangian shows the fastening of the greaves, the leather mounting straps being buckled behind the calf. Under his ringmail he wears a thick woollen tunic with triangular gussets for additional width. To carry his personal belongings he has a pouch fastened with a horn toggle slung from his belt; it might carry flint, steel and tinder as well as a spoon and a cup.

Bows and Bowmen

(Left) Originally the bow was a weapon for hunting, and it was probably to be found in most Viking households. The bow pictured here is typical for the Viking period. Made from a single straight wooden stave (i.e. not glued together from several layers), it shows a D-shaped cross-section with the flat side pointing to the front, and is tapered at the ends. The bowstring is made of a strong twisted cord of hemp or flax. Our bowman wears a simple cap, woollen tunic and trousers, leg wrappings and leather shoes, with a belt for his knife, pouch and quiver.

(Right) This reconstruction shows several different methods of stringing a bow. Like their modern counterparts, bows of the Viking age were delicate instruments needing careful maintenance and handling; exposure to damp or long periods of strong sunlight weakened the wood. This group of bowmen are preparing for battle, with arrows stuck in the ground for immediate use. Note their simple clothing and sidearms.

owmen were the "artillery" of the early Middle Ages, and could be used effectively out to a range of about 200 metres. Like most cutting and stabbing weapons the bow had evolved, and remained in daily use, as a weapon for hunting, but it could equally be used in war. Bows were made of yew, ash or elm and ranged from about 1.6 to 2m (5.2 to 6.5ft) in length. A good example of a Viking bow was found during the excavations at Haithabu. It is of yew, 1.915m (6.2ft) long, and has a "draw weight" of 40.8kg (90lbs); similar bows made of elm were also found at Haithabu. Apparently some bows had a reinforcing wrapping of linen, leather, or even strips of sinew.

The finds at Haithabu also included arrows. The shafts were apparently 70cm-80cm (27.5ins-31.5ins) in length and 8mm-10mm (0.31in-0.39in) in diameter, and already carried the three-feather fletchings which stabilise an arrow's flight by spinning it. Apart from blunt wooden tips as used for practice and for hunting small game a wide variety of iron arrowheads have been found all over Europe, as different in shape as their intended use requires. Among many other shapes there are long, narrow heads which could pierce mail, and others with heads divided to carry plugs of burning tow or other inflammable materials.

Apart from his bow the Viking archer probably carried only a knife or sax, and for sake of easy movement he was unarmoured. Although a bow was not the cheapest of weapons, there is written evidence suggesting that bowmen were usually too poor to afford sword, helmet and armour. But the sagas also speak of great heroes who preferred the bow to any other weapon. The tale of the battle of Svöldr mentions one Einar Tambarskelve, who stood beside King Olaf Tryggvasson. After he had narrowly missed Eric Haakonsson, a leader of the enemy, his bow was broken by an arrow hit. Olaf asked him what had burst with such a noise: he replied, "It was Norway, Sire, that sprang from your hands."

The archers' place in northern European battles of the early Middle Ages seems usually to have been directly behind the ranks of swordsmen and axemen, and they seem to have shot at the enemy "indirectly", i.e. at a high angle to fall into the enemy mass. The battle of Hastings is a good example of their importance: here the Norman bowmen finally broke up the Saxon defensive formation, which had defied cavalry attacks, by dropping arrows into it from above. (It may be significant that of the arrow strikes depicted in the Bayeux Tapestry about one in four are head wounds.) We also know from other references that before close combat began the bowmen of both

(OVERLEAF) The value of archery in any battle larger than a skirmish between handfuls of men depends on the co-ordinated impact of a number of bowmen shooting together. Before closing in hand-to-hand combat armies of the Viking age usually deployed bowmen and threw light axes and javelins. Norwegian and Swedish laws of the period specify that every levied warrior of the *leding* was supposed to bring his own bow and arrows when taking the field.

attackers and defenders often shot at the enemy to thin them out or goad them into unwisely breaking formation.

Archers carried their arrows in quivers which (in contradiction of so many "Robin Hood" fantasies) were slung at the waist and not across the back - this allows much quicker reloading. It was not uncommon to thrust the arrows under the belt without a quiver, or even to stick them into the ground ready to hand. Arrows were often picked up and shot back during a battle.

Just as, say, reading and writing are today automatically mastered by virtually everybody, we can assume that during the early Middle Ages most people were familiar with the use of bow and arrow and practised it from an early age by hunting.

(Left) Archaeological evidence suggests that the force needed to draw a Viking bow was around 40kg (90lbs) - a "draw weight" comparable to that of later medieval long-bows, and one which imparted to the arrow a short range penetrating power suffi-cient to penetrate ringmail and thin wooden shields. After fitting the arrow to the string the archer draws the bow while lifting it, until the drawing hand reaches his cheek; he then looses quickly - holding a drawn bow tires the archer and impairs his aim.

(Below) These three arrow-heads have socket fittings to take the shaft. The upper two are barbed - one of them massively - to make them difficult to pull out of the wound without doing further damage. The lower one is the head of a fire arrow with, in this case, a wickerwork holder for oiled tow which would be set alight immediately before shooting.

(Below) An alternative to the socketed head was the tanged head, forged in one piece with a spike which was driven into the end of the shaft. Both the heads and the fletchings of arrows were doubly secured, by glues such as birch-pitch and by strong thread whip-ping. Although the fashioning of arrows was thought to be a pastime fit for a warrior, in fact it seems often to have been done by the women of the household. This arrow-head shows a cruciform section.

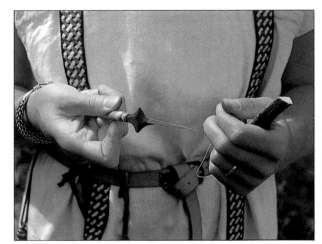

(Left) This bowman carries his quiver at his belt - the normal position throughout Europe over several centuries; a quiver could carry up to 40 arrows, and when these had been shot off it was common to pick up enemy arrows and shoot them back. Our bowman wears a gambeson, and is thus rather more heavily equipped than the norm. On the Bayeux Tapestry only one of many depicted bowmen wears mail, all the others having only a tunic. Although inferior to armoured warriors in hand-to-hand combat, each archer could theoretically control several enemies at a distance, since his arrows could pierce their armour and shields and he could shoot a shaft every few seconds.

(Below) There is no evidence allowing the exact reconstruction of a Viking "shooting tab" to protect the bowman's drawing fingers from the cutting of the bowstring, but we may assume its use; without such protection the repeated drawing of a 40kg bow would become a torture, even to long-practised men with calloused hands.

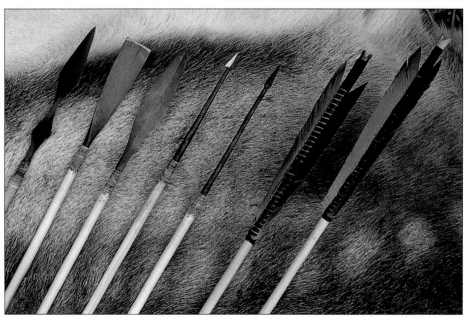

(Left) Details of several arrowheads and two nocks, typical of examples found all over northern Europe. (Left to right) The cruciform head illustrated opposite, its two blades set at right angles; two broad, flat heads, one chisel-shaped and one conventional - these make long, deep wounds which cut muscle and cause great loss of blood; and two sharply pointed pyramid section heads - their impact concentrated into a tiny area, they can burst open the rings of mail. For hunting birds and small game there were also arrows with ball-shaped wooden tips, which brought down the quarry by impact without tearing up the flesh.

41

Rus - The Vikings in the East

Viking traders, mainly from Sweden, reached Byzantium via the Baltic Sea, the Neva, Lake Ladoga, the Volkov, and Lake Ilmen; from there the ships had to be dragged or rolled on logs over a portage to be launched again on the Lovat, sailing on down the Dniepr and finally into the Black Sea. The Vikings even reached the Caspian Sea and Baghdad by travelling via Stavaja Ladoga and Novgorod to reach the Volga.

The eastwards-questing Vikings started to settle along these trading routes, and quickly conquered the local populations. Kiev, for example, originally a Slavic foundation, was ruled by Vikings from 858, and every year traders assembled there before making the journey to Byzantium together.

(**Left**) The Viking routes to the east were long and arduous, and crossed areas populated by nomadic warriors; the warrior- traders had to be capable of defending themselves. Our Rus is one of the richer traders. He wears two tunics over his "Turkish" trousers, an undertunic of linen and an upper tunic made from Friesian wool cloth; both are finely woven and dyed. His leather cap and his coat are trimmed with fur, and he wears high leather boots. He carries a brass-decorated axe - used both as a tool and a weapon in the wild Russian interior - and a decorated horn and pouches complete his belongings.

(**Above**) These high boots fastened with leather toggles are reconstructed from originals found at Ladoga and Haithabu. His legs are covered with cloth wrappings up to the knee.

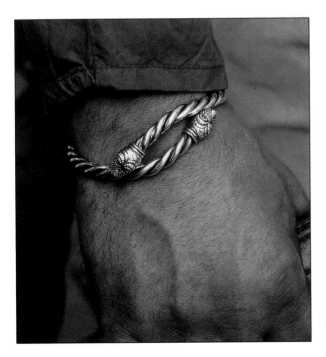

(**Left**) Bracelets like the one illustrated here were worn by both men and women; they served not only as jewellery but also as currency. For this purpose they could even be hacked to pieces if small amounts of silver were needed. Often the twisted silver wires were decorated with animal head motifs; some finds are also made from different precious metals, e.g. combinations of silver with bronze or gold.

The Rus - as the Slavs called the Vikings - undertook these long, arduous river voyages not only for trading reasons: fleets of warships also carried them south and east on raiding expeditions. The Vikings and their ancestors had been exploring these rivers since the 7th century, but their first major attacks were recorded in 852, when a Swedish army demanded high danegeld from the inhabitants of Novgorod. Two failed raids on Miklagard, as the Vikings called Byzantium, also started out from Kiev in about 900, and more followed in 907, 941 and 944.

By this period the Vikings were already mixing with the local Slav population and assimilating to their

43

(Left) Although many depictions show Vikings with simple leather caps we can assume that fur trimming was common. At Birka, a centre for Swedish trade with the east, fragments of fur and leather were found which may have come from a leather cap like this. Coats can be reconstructed from textile finds at Haithabu and from frequent depictions, e.g. on the plates of the helmets found at Välsgarde. Worn by the wealthier sort, they did not have fastenings and were closed with the waist belt.

(Below) The original pattern for these trousers most likely came from the east, but the fashion quickly conquered Scandinavia. Arabian traders nicknamed the Vikings "the people with the trousers made from 100 spans of cloth", suggesting that they were well known for needing large amounts of fabric to make such garments. The legs were gathered into a band slightly below the knee. Note the leather boots, this pair fastened with horn toggles.

culture. The name Rus lived on, as it does today in "Russia"; it may be derived from the Swedish name Roslagen, an area near Stockholm, or equally from the Scandinavian word for "rowing" - often necessary on the eastern rivers. As they did in other areas of settlement, the eastern Vikings often copied local ways and fashions in dress. It is probable that the wide "Turkish" trousers which slowly became common in Scandinavia have their origin in the eastern settlements. But the Vikings also left their marks in Russia; archaeologists have found Viking cemeteries near Smolensk, Kiev, Grezdowa and Novgorod.

The Vikings who travelled east - so-called "traders with the sword" - often collected their trade goods along the way by looting and taking Slavs as prisoners, to exchange for silver, spices and salt. Apart from slaves they offered honey, wax, weapons and furs. An intense trade is also proved by the many items of obviously eastern origin that have been found in Scandinavia - among them a small Buddha statue, and a mosque-shaped basin.

(**Left**) This pouch is closed with a leather toggle and fixed to the belt with two straps. It would carry the trader's items of daily use such as a purse and small scales. The rich decoration shows a beast fighting with a snake which has wound around its head and body; head and tail run into leaved branches, a feature common to motifs of the Mammen style. The original pattern was found on a memorial stone set up by King Harald for his parents at Jellinge.

(**Below**) This pouch is decorated in the manner of Jellinge, another of the many identified Viking decorative styles; it is characterised by heads pictured in profile, spiral shapes, S- shaped bodies with decorating ribbons and branch-like protrusions. Purses like this, both decorated and undecorated and in many sizes, have been found in all areas of Viking settlement.

(**Right**) This Rus, obviously less wealthy, wears the wide trousers in coarser material and less bright colouring. His cap is made from felt with fur trim. Instead of a coat he wears a caped hood against the cold.

Viking Battle Tactics

The Vikings initially gained the decisive advantage over their opponents by surprise attacks. Their raiding parties usually landed over sea beaches or after slipping up river estuaries under cover of darkness or bad weather. The old Roman concept of the "standing army" had quite disappeared from northern Europe since the 5th century; in the face of these hit-and-run raids the local Friesians, Anglo-Saxons or Franks had no time to identify the threat and assemble large defensive forces. The targets of these attacks were also picked to guarantee success, especially the monasteries - although often used as depositories of treasure, these were badly guarded.

At first these local plundering raids were mounted by only a few score men in a handful of ships. However, with the spreading reports of their success, and with the simultaneous appearance of more powerful and unified kingdoms in Norway and Denmark, larger and larger Viking armies landed and stayed ashore longer, eventually over-wintering and later settling for good in their captured territory. Often they caught horses locally to give themselves greater mobility and range. This was the method by which Vikings from the occupied Anglo-Saxon province of East Anglia attacked York in 866.

From 850 Danish Vikings began to stay in England during the winter, taking danegeld in return for promises to keep the peace. Kent paid a large sum in 865, but was nevertheless the victim of a great raid soon afterwards. After 870 the Vikings ruled a great swathe of middle England from coast to coast; for generations various Anglo-Saxon leaders tried to recapture this so-called Danelaw, with varying fortunes. These attempts often led to open field battles, like Brunanburh in 937 and Maldon in 991, where the Vikings proved that they were equal to pitched battles on dry land. Brunanburh is of special interest because it saw Vikings fight on both sides: an Anglo-Saxon army with support from Danish mercenaries met Norwegian rebel lords from Ireland and the eastern Danelaw.

Field battles in northern and western Europe were mainly fought on foot in the early Middle Ages; the battlefield use of mounted troops was rare before the 11th century, although the Franks did have some good quality cavalry. (Such troops were an important element of Byzantine armies in southern and eastern Europe throughout our period.) The Vikings themselves saw the horse as a means of transport and communication. They were defeated by, e.g., the Franks at Saucourt in 881, and the Byzantines at Slistria in 972 because of the superiority of the opposing cavalry. There is no rule without its exceptions, however: in 888 the Vikings themselves deployed horsemen at Monfaucon in France, and in 968 at the battle of Solcoit in Ireland there is written evidence of Viking cavalry.

Sometimes the time and place of a battle were actually settled beforehand, and the limits of the agreed battlefield marked by hazel branch fencing. To leave this field or to break the arrangement was thought dishonourable, as was the pillaging of the enemy's lands once the challenge had been accepted but

(Left) The shield wall was the basic formation in Viking age battles; spear thrusts and blows with sword and axe were delivered over the overlapping shields. The formation illustrated here is advancing, and the warriors hit the rims of their shields with their weapons to demoralise the enemy - a common practice of the time, which makes a deafening noise. Viking shields are thought to have been painted in various solid colours or simple geometrical patterns, red being the most often mentioned, followed by yellow, black, white, green and blue.

(**Right**) Warriors stood shoulder to shoulder as they came together, and as soon as the two shield walls clashed each side tried to break through. The pressure on the front ranks was sometimes so great that dead men could not fall, but were swept along held upright in the crush. If one side broke through they tried to widen the gap; at this point formations broke up, with small groups and individuals fighting one another as defeat turned into rout.

before battle was joined; the Anglo-Saxons sometimes made use of this custom to win time to assemble their forces, as at Brunanburh.

The shield wall

The main battle formation was the "shield wall" or *skjaldborg*. The warriors stood side by side and held their shields rim to rim, or even overlapping; but overlapping the shields does not allow for wide swings with sword or axe, so the front rank were perhaps limited to thrusting or parrying the opponents' spears. Behind the shield-bearers stood spearmen and warriors with long axes, to strike and thrust over the shoulders of their front rank; the terrain could be decisive, the side holding the higher ground having an advantage. Depending on the size of the army there might be several shield walls one behind the other.

There is evidence to suggest that javelin-throwers and bowmen were deployed both before and after the armies made contact, to create weak spots in the opposing shield wall. Then the front ranks would clash together, the warriors thrusting and hacking at each other until one side managed to break through. In the course of this mêlée it seems probable that the gaps between the shields opened up somewhat as individuals traded axe and sword blows. Weak spots might be attacked with a special wedge-shaped formation known as *svynfylking*, in which two warriors formed the point, three the second row, five a third row, and so on; the warriors at the outside carried overlapping shields and the spearmen inside thrust over them as they forced their way forward.

If the integrity of a shield wall was decisively broken it was not unusual for the losing force to dissolve into chaos. Now was the moment when the leader had to show his ability and force of character by rallying and regrouping his warriors, or by bringing in reinforcements which he had withheld up to then. The early medieval Viking army included three types of fighting men: the individual freeborn man who was obliged to do service when summoned; the wealthier hersir who owed allegiance to a jarl (or later to a king), and who brought with him other armed men from his lands; and the leader's sworn bodyguard of retainers, whom he maintained permanently at his own expense. The main target in battle was the leader of the opposing army; if he was killed the common warrior was considered free of his duty, and normally these men - who were hardly trained - were quickly cut down if they did not flee the field. However, honour demanded that the leader's sworn liegemen fight on around him until they too fell.

Sea fights

The sea battles of the Vikings were fought according to the same principles as battles on land. Each side roped most of their ships together side by side to make a platform on which to form a shield wall. The attackers tried to storm this platform, as e.g. in the battles of Hafrsfjord in 872, Svöldr in 1000 and Nissa in 1062. Ship after ship was taken and then detached from the formation to drift away. Both fleets used to keep some ships outside the formation to manoeuvre;

these were used to attack the enemy by going alongside and boarding, in a hailstorm of arrows, stones and spears from both sides. If the defenders succeeded in killing the attacking rowers, or if the oars of the attacking ship were broken, the attack often failed through inability to manoeuver. However, the elements of a real naval battle of the Classical age - outmanoeuvering, ramming, forcing the opponent to sail against the wind, or the use of catapults - were unknown among the Vikings. Most sea battles took place in quiet coastal waters or river mouths, where there was no space for such tactics.

Viking armies

The size of Viking armies varied enormously, growing steadily between the late 8th and 11th centuries. An Anglo-Saxon manuscript of the pre-Viking age calls a group of 35 or more warriors an "army", and we can assume that the first Viking raids were performed by such small bands. Even later battle descriptions rarely mention the number of men; the size of a Viking force was usually given in ships, and the number of crew members on a ship could vary according to the number of oars. The quoted strengths for the siege of Paris in 886 - 40,000 men and 700 ships - give an average of just under 60 oars per ship; but crew sizes must have varied (and anyway, all figures from early sources should be treated as "impressionist" rather than mathematically exact).

The early raids were usually led by a local leader, with the aim of capturing land at home or valuable booty and slaves abroad. His crews were recruited from men of the same family or clan and perhaps some neighbours, all of them bringing their own equipment, and hoping for eventual reward in the form of shared plunder. Often they were both warriors and traders, selling at one place what they had looted from another. They usually had an agreed leader, but important decisions were often discussed

(Above) The Vikings seem seldom to have attempted to take fortified positions; but an attack with scaling ladders, as reconstructed here, is not unlikely. We know that Viking armies took cities like York, Paris and Bremen, although it is questionable whether these fell to true assaults or surrendered after sieges. The common fortifications of the Viking age were walls and enclosed encampments protected by wooden palisades.

(Left) At the beginning of the 9th century a small group of raiders like this, making a surprise attack on a poorly defended village or monastery, was already being termed an "army" - remember that few of their victims had ever before seen any large armed force. However, numbers increased, and Hardrada led at least 10,000 to England in 1066. The high proportion of spearmen is quite authentic; a spear was much cheaper than a sword, and more generally useful. The two bare-chested men at the front may be berserkers.

Berserkers

Many sagas describe the exploits of *berserkirs* or *ulfhednar*. These terms - derived from "bear-shirt" and "wolf-coat" respectively - were used of warriors who, when going into battle, fell into a rage amounting to a state of possession which gave them superhuman strength and made them oblivious of wounds. This condition was apparently hereditary; it may have been associated with epilepsy, perhaps aggravated by a belief in possession by animal spirits (thus the reference to animal skins) or even by drug abuse. The pagan Vikings believed that berserkers were touched by Odin, and they were greatly valued as members of kings' bodyguards; the later, Christian Vikings strongly disapproved of them. Typical signs of a berserk rage were the tearing off of armour and clothes, and the biting of the shield rim - a feature seen among the carved warriors in the 12th century chess set found on the Isle of Lewis.

among the whole group. Some might be as young as 15 or even 12 years when they first went a-viking; every boy learned strength, dexterity and swiftness from an early age by hunting, and the fighting skills taught by his father were practised with his friends.

(Below) This free peasant, fulfilling his duty to the *leding* or levy, would probably prefer to be at home tending his farm. His clothing and equipment are typical for the poor warriors who formed the main body of the Viking armies; he has no protection except for his shield, which he has strapped to his back, and his weapons are a spear and some javelins. He looks as if he is contemplating one of the stanzas from the *Havamal*, a collection of Viking proverbs, which reads: *"Better living than not living. / Only the living hold wealth. / I saw a fire blaze up in a rich man's home, / But death stood outside the door."*

(Above) The dead and wounded were routinely plundered after battle, and sometimes even while the fighting was still going on. Money and jewellery would have been much less common loot than armour and weapons; the Bayeux Tapestry shows corpses stripped to the skin. This humble warrior seems likely to fulfill at least the modest ambition of going home wearing a pair of shoes.

The uniting of Norwegian and Danish territories into kingdoms changed the structure of armies. For national defence the Scandinavian kingdoms adopted the so-called *leding* or levy: a conscription system whereby every free man owning land had to provide men, equipment, ships and weapons, the numbers depending on the size of his holding. Later the leding was replaced by a tax from which professional soldiers were paid. The king led his forces and was guarded by the *hird*, his personal bodyguard, every man of which had sworn allegiance to him.

Even given a necessary scepticism over quoted figures, genuinely large armies were not uncommon in the later Viking age. The Norsemen are supposed to have lost at least 8,000 men at Saucourt in 881. The army led by King Harald Hadrada to defeat at Stamford Bridge in 1066 had allegedly crossed in between 240 and 300 ships. Olaf Tryggvasson raided Maldon in 991 with a fleet of 93 ships, to make money to finance his attempt on the Norwegian 49

(Left) Before engaging in hand-to-hand combat both sides tried to weaken the enemy ranks with arrows and javelins. Depictions on jewellery and stones show warriors with shield and spear carrying additional short javelins in their shield hand.

throne. Here the army was made up from groups of hersir owing allegiance to a jarl who, in his turn, owed allegiance to the king.

On occasion some kings - e.g. Harald Bluetooth - would provide a proportion of their troops with weapons and even armour. The raising of mercenary troops was another factor; a good example is the army of Thorkel the Great, serving only themselves and the man who paid best.

Fortifications

There are some known Viking age fortifications, like the "wall castles" (defensive enclosures) at Fyrkat, Aggersborg, Trelleborg and Nonnebakken, and of course the Danewerk. This great earthwork in southern Jutland - 2m high by 12m wide (6.5ft by 39ft), and revetted with timber - connected natural obstacles with each other to provide protection against the Slavs and German raiders. The first parts of this system had been built by 737, and the last work is dated to 968. In the overall length of 30km (18.6 miles) there was only one gate, through which ran the road to Viborg. Haithabu, one of the most important trading cities of the age, was in the vicinity of the Danewerk. But even the Danewerk could not prevent the Germans under Emperor Otto II from conquering the greater part of southern Denmark in 974 (they were driven out again in 983).

The four Viking fortresses named above were all built in the second half of the 10th century and are all similar in construction, only the size varying. Each features a circular wall and ditch, and two main roads cutting the interior into quarters. At Trelleborg, Fyrkat and Nonnebakken there were 16 large longhouses in four symmetrical groups; Aggersborg has twice the diameter of the others and three times as many buildings. Outside the main walls there were additional enclosures and buildings, the arrangement varying from site to site. Although a military use cannot be ignored, the main purpose of these fortified sites seems to have been the protection of the local population, and equally to provide suitable accomodation for the Danish king's representatives. They might also have been used to house groups of warriors assembled for training or for a campaign, however.

(Right) "Deliver us, O Lord, from the fury of the Norsemen. . ." This Viking's shield already shows the marks of battle; shields were made thin for lightness, and presumably did not last longer than one or two battles. The metal boss could be reused, and wood and rawhide would have been cheap and plentiful.

(**Left above**) If they were attacked with arrows or light spears the Vikings could take cover behind their shields, arranging them as shown here; there are clear references to such tactics in both land and sea battles. With enough men gathered, some could even hold their shields over the heads of the group - rowers were protected in this way when closing to board at sea. The photos in this chapter show the broad variety of shield designs.

(**Above**) The two battle lines meeting here both show a high proportion of spears. During this early stage of a battle warriors armed with sword or axe could do little more than try to parry enemy spear thrusts from behind the shield wall, while their own spearmen tried to create gaps in the enemy's shield wall for exploitation by swordsmen and axemen.

(**Right**) The first and third shields in this wall show clearly their construction from individual planks. The fourth shows the leather rim binding sewn on, and on the third the rawhide is nailed - though in those days of individual hand forging nails would have been relatively expensive.

Simple colour washes were presumably more common than complex motifs, but the latter are found in some sources. The shields from the Gokstad ship find were painted plain black or yellow; the Oseberg Tapestry shows one with a cross design; those of St.Olaf's men supposedly bore crosses in red and blue on white; and Gotland picture stones show many with radial wavy lines or divisions.

Viking Mercenaries

In 9th and 10th century Scandinavia there are descriptions of brotherhoods of mercenaries - *Vikinge-lag* - who lived together under special codes of conduct. These experienced fighters did not seek to take land on their own account, but hired themselves out for paid military service. One of the most famous of these brotherhoods were the *Jomsvikinge-lag* or Jomsvikings, who were probably established in the fortified camp and harbour of Jomsburg - today's Wollind, at the mouth of the Oder in Wendland - in the 980s by the exiled Harald Bluetooth of Denmark. Led by one Jarl Sigvald, a Scanian noble, they quickly inspired the admiration of minstrels, and they are mentioned in accounts of Viking battles.

According to later sagas, a Jomsviking had to be between 18 and 50 years of age and stronger than the average warrior. When living at Jomsburg the members of the brotherhood were expected to keep the peace among themselves, submitting any serious dispute for judgement by the commander. They were not to leave for more than three days without permission; women were not allowed inside Jomsburg, and no Jomsviking was allowed to take a woman or child prisoner. All loot was divided equally between the brotherhood; and members were expected to avenge each other's deaths. They were not to show any signs of fear in battle, and were only permitted to retreat if obviously outnumbered (Sigvald is described as a "prudent" man). Violation of these laws meant immediate expulsion.

The Jomsvikings were the subject of their own saga, which was written down in Iceland in about 1200. They are also mentioned in other sagas: that of King Olaf Tryggvasson states that hiring them was a question of prestige (although they seem to have been on the losing side in a number of important battles). The brotherhood was fading away by about 1010, and the remnant was destroyed by King Magnus of Norway in 1043.

(Above) The pommel and guard of this sword show rich silver and bronze inlays, and the scabbard has decorated fittings. The sagas often mention individual weapons being named, sometimes in reference to special details of the weapon but usually to invoke success in battle: some examples are *Shield-Notcher, Foot-Biter, Head-Reddener, Redbeak* and *Bluetongue*.

(Left & below) A spangenhelm with a long nasal and a mail neckguard, and a leather gambeson, make up the armour of this warrior taking a refreshment break. There is no archaeological evidence for the leather lining to the neckguard, but some figures in the Bayeux Tapestry show lines which might suggest it. He is armed with a sword and a sax and his shield is slung on his back. Note that this gambeson only covers the torso and offers insufficient protection in battle. The description of the battle of Stamford Bridge tells us that Vikings would sometimes leave their heavy mail on board ship if they needed to move fast across country, or might even take it off in battle if frustrated by its weight.

Ships and Seafaring

The Vikings were outstanding shipbuilders, navigators and sailors. In other European countries seafaring generally meant skirting along the coasts; but the Vikings made direct crossings of the North Sea and Baltic, and ventured far out across the North Atlantic. Today any sailor can check his position to within a few metres thanks to GPS; our 19th century great-grandfathers could con themselves around the globe with sextant and chronometer; but it seems miraculous to us that a Viking captain, braving some of the world's roughest seas without instruments or charts, ever reached his destination. Yet Viking navigation was reliable enough for regular crossings to Iceland and Greenland, providing the new colonies with all the supplies upon which they depended for survival.

Sometimes, inevitably, a captain would miss his landfall - like Bjarni Herjolfsson, whose supply voyage to Greenland in about 985 went astray, carrying him on to North America. He probably sighted the coast of Newfoundland; he did not land, but made his way back to Greenland. Some years later Leif Ericsson, inspired by Bjarni's story, led an expedition to try to settle this promising new country of "Vinland".

Frustratingly, we do not know how the Vikings navigated the high seas, but the most likely guess is that they sailed on a fixed latitude until they reached a coast and then turned north or south. In the areas where the Vikings sailed the North Star can always be seen, and to keep the latitude they only had to make sure that it stayed at the same height above the horizon. The distance covered could be roughly calculated from elapsed time and estimated speed. These assumptions are based on the fact that in the sagas ships usually lose their way in bad weather, i.e. when the North Star was hidden for long periods, the direction of the wind changed quickly, or strong winds carried the ship along faster than estimated.

Viking ship finds

Even today Viking ships fascinate us by their elegant lines as much as by their epic voyages. Hardly any book on the subject appears without a frontal view of the vessel found at Gokstad in 1880 (this was neither

(Left) A sight which struck terror throughout Europe in the 9th and 10th centuries: a Viking ship approaching the beach. Although the reconstructions illustrated here are necessarily of small vessels, this angle shows to advantage the high prow and low gunwale characteristic of all sizes. With a top speed of about 11 knots (12.6mph, 20kmh) a ship like this could make nearly 500km (310 miles) in a single day on the open sea, where sailing continued day and night.

(Right) The side-mounted rudder was fixed to the uppermost plank at the right rear; the horizontal tiller bar could be controlled by a single helmsman. The rudder was deeper than the keel, and on approaching the beach it was simply taken aboard - our picture shows this procedure. It was held in position by a leather strap running through slits in the hull. Note also the clinker construction of the hull, with each row of planks nailed to overlap the one below.

(Left) The reconstructed rigging; note also the characteristic hanging of the crew's shields along the gunwales, confirmed by many depictions and by archaeology. The front and rear stays run to the prow and stern, the shrouds to the side planks. From the lower corners of the sail ropes run to the deck allowing it to be tightened, and from the tips of the yard two more control the angle of the yard. Viking ships were rigged to sail mainly before the wind or with the wind abeam, but also handled surprisingly well close to the wind.

a trader nor a warship, but probably a kind of yacht or leader's barge). The Gokstad ship, studied in comparison with the Oseberg ship (which was used in a 9th century burial), and the finds in the Roskildefjord at Skuldelev (where several 11th century vessels were scuttled as block-ships), enables us to trace the development of Viking shipbuilding. The general characteristics had already evolved in pre-Viking times, as the Anglo-Saxon ship burials at Sutton Hoo prove; but the Vikings perfected the design.

The sagas mention a variety of names for different types of ships; it is difficult to match names to categories, but the main division was between cargo vessels and warships. The building method was identical for both classes, but the dimensions show that they were meant for different functions.

A warship was built to be swift and manoeuvrable, to carry many men, and to move quickly even without sails. It did not have to be completely ocean-worthy; raids were made in summer, and there was time to wait for good weather if open sea had to be crossed. The speed was achieved by a 7:1 ratio of length to width, manoeuvrability by a curved keel which allowed it to turn around its central axis. To guarantee a high speed without sails there was room for many rowers on a straight deck running along the full length. There were probably so many crewmen that the oars could be manned day and night.

Trading ships were built to give plenty of room for cargo, to be manoeuvered by a small crew, and to cope with bad weather. They were more beamy, with a length-to-width ratio of only 4:1, higher sides, and an open hold in the middle with deck planking and oars at bow and stern only. They were meant to be driven mainly by sails; it must have been tedious to row them with such a small crew. The 16.3m long (53.5ft) Skuldelev 1 - a completely seaworthy trading ship - was manned by about a dozen sailors, whereas the 18m (59ft) warship Skuldelev 2 had a crew of about thirty.

Construction

No matter what the ship's function, the construction techniques were the same; and the most striking feature is that the planking was built directly onto the keel, stem and stern posts with the inner ribs added only later.

The process began with stem and stern posts cut from one treetrunk and a keel cut from a second - always of oak, even when suitable oak trees became scarce and other parts of the ship were built from pine, ash, birch, alder or willow. The planks were then fitted along the keel row after row, each overlapping the one below (i.e. clinker-building). Iron

(Right) During their great raiding voyages through Europe the Vikings often penetrated far up the great rivers; they rowed up the Volga, the Rhine, the Seine, the Loire, the Thames, the Liffey, and many others to plunder inland cities. Most of the time they had to row against the current for days, camping on the banks at night.

(**Above & right**) This picture shows how the keel of a ship was cut from a single trunk; the shipwright uses an adze. Axes, adzes and wedges were the main tools used in shipbuilding; others were gouges to cut caulking grooves into the planks, knives and shaves to fashion the smaller pieces, pliers, and nails (if the planks were nailed together) or augers to drill holes for wooden pegs. Prow and stern posts, and sometimes the upper run of planks, were often decorated with carving.

nails were used in Scandinavia; in the eastern settlements shipbuilders used wooden pegs into which a wedge was hammered. Each row of planks was caulked, in Scandinavia with tarred tow or rope, in Russia with moss and tar. The planks were relatively thin; on the bigger ships they measured about 25mm (1in) below and 43mm (1.7ins) at the waterline, and small skiffs found with the Gokstad ship have 15mm (0.6in) planks. Viking ships were nevertheless strong enough to transport horses.

When the hull was finished the inner construction was added. First ribs were fitted crosswise to the keel, but connected only to the hull; this gave the structure great flexibility to "work" with the waves, but at a price - a Viking ship was never really watertight, and the crew were always having to bale her out. During the early period the ribs were tied to the planks (through extensions left on the planks when they were cut) using spruce roots; later the ribs were nailed to the planks.

Above the ribs horizontal crosstimbers were fitted, connected vertically and horizontally to the hull with L-shaped

57

pieces of wood tied or, later, nailed in place. A second, and on the largest ships a third layer of horizontal timbers could be attached. To these the deck planking was fitted; the deck had no direct connection to the hull, again for flexibility.

The mast was fixed to the keel by means of the "keel pig", a big L-shaped oak block whose vertical piece supported the base of the mast at the front; and a strong horizontal strut, the "mast fish". Comparison of archaeological finds shows steady development; e.g. the keel pig of the Oseberg ship was too small and showed signs of repair, while later ships have bigger keel pigs and even dispense with the mast fish.

Treetrunks were split and wedged apart radially to make planks. Where possible curved and angled parts were cut from naturally shaped timber, along the grain; the keel pig and other L-shaped pieces could be cut from a section of trunk at the junction of a large branch. The most important tools were the axe and adze, and it is fascinating to see how the most exact work was carried out with these simple blades - there is no evidence of sawn timbers.

Sailing

It is difficult to reconstruct the rigging of Viking ships because we only have finds of hulls. Today's reconstructions are based on contemporary depictions such as coins and the Bayeux Tapestry. The mast was probably no longer than could easily be stowed inside the ship. Taking down the mast was quite common, and the construction of the keel pig allowed it to be laid backwards, thus limiting the length of the mast to about half the length of the ship.

Some surviving pictures show shrouds and stays - ropes which support the mast to the sides, front and rear - but the fixings of these ropes cannot be reconstructed. The rectangular sail was fixed at the top to a horizontal spar or yard, the lower edge sometimes being manipulated with another pole called the *beitiass* when sailing close to the wind; it was

(Above) Today we can hardly imagine how the Vikings crossed the Atlantic in open boats like this. Freight ships had at least partial decking at prow and stern but an open central hold; warships had a low deck running along the whole length and gave no shelter at all against the weather. As the crew of a warship probably numbered more than twice the number of oars, and each warrior took along his whole equipment, space must have been very tight. Cargo ships had a smaller number of sailors, but more than half of the ship was filled with trade goods.

(Left) The shallow draught allowed Viking ships to sail close inshore, and raiders took advantage of this to appear suddenly and disappear with equal speed before a defence could be organised. Even the less manoeuverable and deeper-draught trading ships were often beached if the lie of the coast allowed it, as confirmed by the scratches on the keel and planks of the Skuldelev 3 ship find. To beach a ship with such a thin hull - with any hope of its swimming again afterwards - must have taken impressive skill and experience.

(**Left**) The Gokstad ship had T-shaped poles forward and aft of the mast on which the yard could be laid when the sail was taken down; here the sail is reefed to the yard for stowage. If the oars had to be used the sail was most probably always taken down - at such times it was not only useless but actually worked against the rowers.

controlled with ropes running from the tips of the yardarms. Despite the simple rigging sailing against the wind was apparently possible, though if time allowed the captain usually waited for a more favourable wind.

In 1893 a Norwegian captain crossed the Atlantic from Bergen to Newfoundland in a reconstruction of the Gokstad ship, proving that Viking ships really were seaworthy. His reports of the crossing show his astonishment at the sailing qualities of the ship, and record top speeds of 11 knots, i.e. about 20km/h. He also praised the steering. Viking ships had a rudder fitted to the right side of the stern; this makes the ship tend to the left, but the Viking shipwrights gave the rudder a profile similar to an aircraft wing, thus both correcting this bias and also preventing pressure building up on the rudder - even in heavy seas it could be manned by only one helmsman.

These beautiful Viking ships were the result of centuries of experience in shipbuilding and seamanship, and were clearly superior in most respects to the wallowing, barrel-hulled "cogs" that succeeded them. It was their small cargo capacity which led to their replacement during the later Middle Ages by larger but infinitely less graceful vessels.

(**Right**) Small dinghies or skiffs were built following the same principles as ocean-going ships. One obvious difference is the fact that each rower has a pair of oars instead of one. The number of oars gave the type of boat illustrated its name: faering or "four-oared". The number of oars was the common way of describing the size of a ship.

Clothing and Jewellery

Materials and methods

The basic material of Viking clothing was wool. Rich or poor, everyone wore woollen cloth - but the quality varied between different groups in society. Imported cloth was worn to display wealth; Friesian and Anglo-Saxon weaves were particularly desirable. Bright colours might also suggest wealth, as some were usually achieved by difficult dying techniques using expensive, imported raw materials - e.g. indigo and purple. The mass of poorer folk had to be content with cloth which could be woven at home and coloured with the extracts of local plants (though these were varied and versatile - see below).

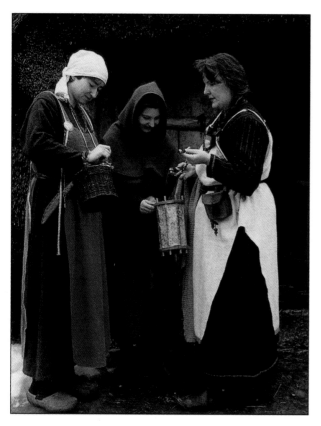

(Above) The women at left and right wear the hangerock or "apron-skirt" over one or more tunics; at centre is a thick winter tunic and a separate caped hood. The basic material throughout was wool of different weights and qualities, though richer women often wore linen undertunics in summer. Woven patterns, such as these stripes (right), were popular. Note the paired brooches fastening the front and back panels of the apron-skirt in front of the shoulders, and braid strips trimming the lower edges of the tunic (right). The lantern - reconstructed from an 11th century original found in Gotland - is made from a wooden frame covered with a pig's bladder, enclosing tallow candles.

Some of the sheep kept in Viking times did not have to be sheared, as they lost their wool through natural moulting; but whether it had to be sheared or only picked up, all the wool had to be cleaned first of all. This was done carefully so that the natural oil was not removed - wool retaining its natural lanoline is easier to comb and spin and is more weatherproof. After cleaning the wool was combed to align the fibres and prepare it for spinning. If a fine yarn was needed to make a tightly woven cloth the short fibres were removed by combing, leaving only the stiffer upper hairs; for a thick felted cloth the shorter fibres would also be spun into the yarn.

The process of spinning twists the fibres to make an endless yarn. From the invention of spinning - perhaps 12,000 years ago - until the invention of the spinning wheel in the 13th century, there was only one tool for this: the hand spindle. The simplest type consisted of a stick; by the Viking age the spindle had acquired a weight fitted to one end to make it twist more evenly.

To spin yarn, some fibres are pulled from a mass of fleece, twisted together to form a starting thread and fixed to the end of the spindle. The spindle is lowered towards the ground, rotating on the end of the lengthening yarn which is created by its twisting motion as more wool is fed on to it through the hands. When the spindle reaches the ground the spinner pauses, winds the new yarn onto it in a spool, fixes the last of this to the top of the spindle again, and repeats the process. The lighter the spindle, the thinner the yarn; but the spindle will not run as long as a heavy one and has to be restarted more often. A heavier spindle runs longer, but the weight makes it more likely that the yarn will break. If the fibres are very short the technique described cannot be used; the spindle has to be rested in a bowl, or simply turned by rolling it over the thigh.

When the yarn had been spun - a tedious and unpopular job - it had to be woven into cloth. Most Viking cloth was woven on vertical weighted looms: simple frames that lean against a wall. Some of the warp or vertical threads are tied to the top of the frame and tightened with weights; others are fixed to a horizontal bar by which they can be pulled to the front. Through the resulting gaps between the two groups of warp threads, the weft or crosswise yarn is threaded, crossing over and under differing numbers of warp threads, and then pushed tight against the edge of the already woven section.

(Left) Poor women like farm workers or the even lower-ranking slaves would probably wear only one simple tunic, and often did not even own a pair of shoes. In summer they would go barefoot, in winter they wrapped leather, fur or pieces of cloth around their feet. Owning a belt buckle and a knife is already the beginnings of relative wealth; the knife also indicates that she is not a slave.

(Right) In contrast, this woman wears richly decorated clothes and jewellery; the style is that of Finland. Over the white tunic she wears a blue apron-skirt of a completely different type from other Scandinavian regions, cut like a Greek *peplos*; also unique to Finland was the true apron worn over it. She has three fine "tortoise" brooches with metal chains and pendants in Finnish style - local finds show brass spiral motifs. Note that her knife, scissors and keys are suspended from the brooches; the pouch seems to hang from a belt, but this is actually the apron string.

The appearance and durability of the cloth depend on how many warp threads the weft crosses before it passes under a warp thread. Viking cloth was mainly woven to give a compromise between durability and softness, not unlike modern denim; this allows a broad variety of weaving patterns, e.g. rhomboids or "herringbone" patterns - the latter a Viking favourite. The warp was usually woven tighter than the weft.

The invention of the so-called horizontal loom, which allowed the groups of warp threads to be moved by a pedal action, brought a four-fold increase in productivity; and the discovery at the Haithabu site of a shaft roll, a part of this type of loom, proves that this invention took place during the Viking age. However, it is questionable whether this new device reached the remoter areas of Viking settlement; even at Haithabu - a relatively cosmopolitan centre of international trade - a single shaft roll find is accompanied by large numbers of weights from the old pattern loom.

After weaving the cloth was often "fulled"; the Vikings favoured a finish similar to modern loden. This procedure lifts the nap to make the cloth "hairy" and gives better protection against rain, and some finds at Haithabu show cloth fulled to such a degree that it almost looks like fur. The Vikings also made woven "fake fur" - *roggvarfeldr*, a shaggy weave incorporating tufts of unspun wool; this was used for cloaks and other garments as well as for trimming the edges of clothing.

Often the cloth or its raw materials were dyed, sometimes with plants which could be picked locally, sometimes with materials imported at great cost. The variety of colours that can be achieved without modern chemical dyes is surprising, and it is quite mistaken to assume that vegetable dyes necessarily produce dull shades. Such "natural" colours are not limited to greens and browns, but include bright yellows, reds and blues. Brighly coloured clothes were worn by whoever could afford them. On the whole, Viking clothing was more sophisticated and made to higher standards than might be expected from looking at the simple tools with which it was made. The finest examples of preserved fabrics count more than 50 threads to the centimetre, and the variety that could be achieved by different weaves, treatments and colourings is impressive.

Apart from wool the Vikings also used linen to some extent; but as this is woven from a plant fibre, it had to compete for scarce fertile land with the plants needed for food, whereas sheep would live in areas that could not be cultivated. To grow linen meant that you had more land than you needed to feed your family, so it was a sign of wealth. Moreover, linen is less warm and thus less versatile than wool; a man who could afford only a few pieces of clothing would not have chosen linen. It can be spun to a very fine thread and gives thin cloth, so it was often used for underwear; a special weaving technique gave it a pleated look which made it outline the figure.

Silk was a prized material throughout Europe during the Viking age - a very expensive luxury which

(Above) Spinning woollen yarn from fleece was one of the never-ending chores of women and children, and one not regarded highly, despite the fact that it demands skill and concentration as well as patience. Note the weight at the lower end of the spindle, ensuring an even spin; this one seems to be made from soapstone, but clay was the most common material. Our spinner wears a linen under-tunic, wool upper tunic and linen *hangerock*. The lower edges of upper tunic and hangerock are hemmed up with an embroidery stitch.

(Above) A vertical weighted loom with work in progress. The vertical warp threads are spanned by loom weights. The horizontal bar rests on the two Y-shaped arms when it is pulled to the front. The upper boom can be rotated in quarter-turns to roll up the finished cloth. The rests for the horizontal bar and the lower boom can be moved up and down the frame by means of pegs. Viking age looms were built for cloth approximately 120cm (47ins) wide.

(Left) A dyer at work; usually the yarn was dyed, not the finished cloth. A high intensity of colouring is not achieved by simply leaving the wool in the dye for a long time, but by several short baths. The result of a dying process depends on many factors, some of them hardly controllable, like the soluble minerals present in local water - the same basic ingredients can give completely different colours with two different "hardnesses" of water.

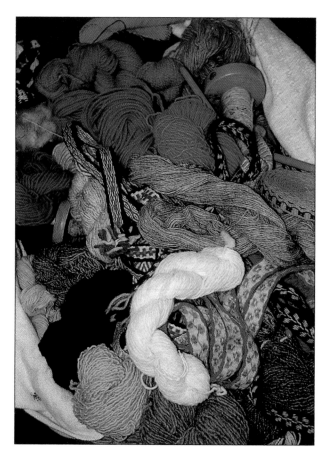

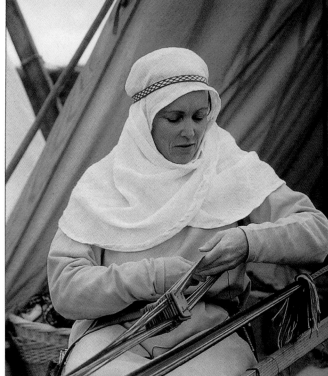

(Above) This woman is making tablet-woven braid. Note the square tablets with a hole in each corner, and how the weaver threads in the weft; the next step will be to push it back with a wooden stick and to turn the whole block of tablets by 90 degrees, in whichever direction is dictated by the pattern. The patterns of tablet-woven braid are simple due to the "short repeat", but an inventive weaver will always be able to think up a new variant.

(Above) All the yarns in this basket were dyed with materials that were known and available in the Viking age; their variety and intensity - especially the reds and yellows - give the lie to our restricted modern ideas about the colours which could be achieved with "natural" ingredients. Combinations of common colouring agents and mineral mordents gave medieval dyers a wide palette of subtle shades, limited only by local availability.

(Below) Some typical examples of tablet-woven braids, clearly showing the short repeat - in all these lengths a change of direction is marked by a vertical symmetrical axis. (Photo courtesy Melanie Donus)

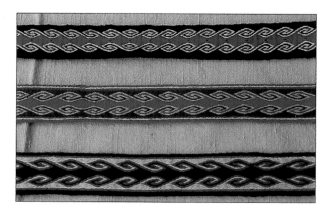

had to be imported over great distances from Asia. Only the very wealthy could afford silk, which was in any case too vulnerable for everyday use in the robust daily lifes of even the richest Vikings. It was most often used for decorative braiding and embroidery; a Haithabu find of a half-finished piece of tablet weaving is believed by archaeologists to have originally included golden wefts and silken warps.

Cotton was worn in the contemporary Byzantine Empire, and had reached southern Spain with the Moors, but there is no evidence for its use in Scandinavian clothing.

Specialist techniques

The Vikings knew two textile techniques which are worth special mention, as they are nearly forgotten today.

Since the early Iron Age, *tablet weaving* was used to make decorative braiding. In this technique the warp does not run over a bar but through holes in the corners of small square tablets made from wood or bone. Rotating these tablets twists the warp into a yarn; many of these tablets laid side by side will give many yarns lying side by side, which are held together by a weft running through. The finished 63

cut straight and with added sleeves. To give more width at the lower edge gussets might be incorporated, sometimes of a contrasting colour. The woman's tunic was ankle length, sometimes long- or half- sleeved, sometimes sleeveless. It was typically worn with a long overgarment made from rectangular lengths of material front and back, joined by straps and brooches at the shoulders (identified for the purposes of this text as an "apron-skirt", for lack of any more descriptive English term).

The man's tunic reached the knee, and was worn over trousers. Trousers seem to have been cut in various shapes: full-length, straight and loose; tighter-fitting in the manner of later medieval hose; knee-length, with separate, cross-gartered leggings below; and - for the relatively wealthy, given the amount of material needed - in the baggy Rus style. These garments, made from woollen cloth and normally loose enough for easy movement, were often the only clothing a Viking owned apart from a simple woollen cloak, and a belt to which small possessions might be slung.

(Above) In contrast to most warriors or traders pictured in this book, this labourer is obviously poor; but he is wearing a knife, so cannot be a slave. Apart from some good luck charms dangling from a leather thong around his neck, this seems to be his only possesion. He does not own shoes, and his clothes are made from undyed cloth.

(Below) This woman's long coat was a common female garment. She protects herself from the winter cold by several layers of clothing; under the coat the lower edges of an undertunic, a tunic and an apron-skirt can be seen. The belt she uses to close the coat also serves to hold knife, scissors, pouch and drinking horn; the coat is also fastened at the throat with a brooch. Just visible at the right wrist is one of the twisted silver bracelets which typically served both as jewellery and currency.

braid will show the colour of the uppermost thread; if threads of different colours are used in the same tablet, patterns can be made. While most examples show repeating geometrical or wavy shapes, quite complex patterns can be produced if the direction in which the tablets are rotated is changed at planned intervals - flowers, figures, even Viking ships.

Knitting and crocheting were unknown to the Vikings, but to make cloth which had to be elastic - e.g. for stockings - they used a technique called *naalbinding*. A long thread is laid into loops with a thick needle which is threaded through the last row of loops, giving a result not unlike knitted work. Even large garments such as cloaks could be made in this fashion, but are thought to have been uncommon.

Clothing

The basic garment for both men and women in the early Middle Ages was the tunic, a simple shirt-shape

Signs of relative wealth might include an undertunic of pleated linen, and outer garments tailored to a tighter fit. The wealthy Viking woman might combine a linen undertunic with a tight apron-skirt and a coat-like outer tunic. Her husband might wear an outer tunic cut to fit at the chest, a thigh-length cloak with overlapping front, and trousers confined by puttee-like leg wrappings below the knee.

For protection against bad weather there were cloaks and tunics of fulled wool, or cowls - hoods with capes covering the neck and upper chest. Some special winter clothing was doubled, and sometimes even had a filling of down.

As mentioned above, a wide variety of coloured dyes were used, the wealthier sort displaying imported fabrics or expensive colours, the poorer wearing homespun either undyed or coloured with readily available agents (e.g. a Haithabu find dyed dark brown with walnut, which also had a disinfecting property). Viking clothing was often decorated at the lower edges either with applied braiding or with embroidery, and outer clothing was often trimmed with fur; the degree of decoration, too, was an indicator of wealth.

The same was true of the style and material of the brooches and pins used to fasten the garments. A rich Viking wore cloak brooches of gold or silver at shoulder or hip, and his wife fixed her apron-skirt with a pair of richly decorated brooches linked by chains or beads; but a poor man would carve a button from wood or horn. The design and material of the belt, its buckle and any metal strap end also depended upon the owner's resources.

The typical Viking shoe was an ankle-high "turn-shoe" fastened with laces at the side, and usually made from goatskin. Higher boots were also worn, some with ankle flaps fastened by toggles. Footwear was sometimes decorated with embroidery.

Jewellery

Jewellery was a flourishing trade. Pieces made by silversmiths and goldsmiths, bronze casters, bone carvers and glass bead makers were used for display, as a store of wealth and as currency. Viking age Scandinavia had few coins; payment was often by barter, and if no exchange of goods could be agreed then payment could be made with an appropriate amount of precious metal - especially the necklaces and bracelets typical of the period, either whole or cut into smaller pieces. There was clearly no hesitation about cutting up such "works of art"; so many Viking hoards contain parts of larger artefacts which have been broken up that archaeologists use the specific term "hacksilver".

Although some of it was made to be broken up and melted down, Viking jewellery shows a high standard of craftsmanship, employing nearly all techniques that are still in use today. The pieces were cast or hammered from a flat piece, the surfaces decorated with engraving, filigree work or niello inlay - the only unknown technique seems to have been enamelling. Many bronze and silver artefacts were gilded. Through their widespread trading the Vikings had contact with many other cultures, and such influences are evident in their jewellery. The Celtic motif of entwined beasts was imported from Ireland, but the Vikings substituted their beloved dragons for the human and dog figures of most Irish originals. Frankish influence can be seen in the trefoil brooches made mainly in Denmark; in Gotland Slavic forms were copied.

Apart from their functions as decoration and means of exchange, many pieces obviously had everyday uses. Pins, clasps and brooches were needed to keep garments together, the most striking being the large "tortoise" brooches with which Viking women fastened their apron-skirts. These were always in matching pairs, often linked by chains of glass beads.

(Below) Children's clothes were no different from those of adults; these boys wear the same combination of tunic, trousers and cloak as their fathers, although less decorative. It is likely that the clothes of fast-growing young children were hardly ever dyed - that the boy at right wears coloured clothes and even leather shoes shows that his parents must be wealthy. The embroidery at the edges of his cloak serves to fix the hem, whereas that of the cloak at left is purely decorative.

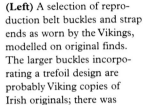

(Left) A selection of reproduction belt buckles and strap ends as worn by the Vikings, modelled on original finds. The larger buckles incorporating a trefoil design are probably Viking copies of Irish originals; there was much trade and contact between Norway and the Irish settlements, originally via the Orkneys and the Hebrides. Viking belts often had not only a buckle and strap end but also belt mounts - small metal plates punched into the leather strap.

Trefoil brooches were used by women to fasten a short, shawl-like cape; cloaks were fastened with a simple pin, a big ring pin, or a silver or bronze brooch.

Another piece of jewellery in everyday use was the amulet, meant to protect the bearer and bring him good luck. The most famous contemporary charm is the "Thor's hammer", made from a variety of materials and in many styles - in bronze, silver or gold, and/or combined with a chain - and apart from the well-known abstract form there are also miniature copies of real hammers. Other types of amulets are also known. Christian Vikings wore crosses; a small amber leg found at Haithabu is thought to be a good luck charm; and there are finds of amber axeheads and coiled snakes from Scandinavia, Ireland and the Danelaw.

(Left) Children making felt balls. Felt is related to loden, but the fibres are fulled without spinning and weaving them first. Rubbing wool fibres in soapy water and beating them into a mass eventually produces, after drying, sheets of material which can be handled like woven cloth. The Vikings made both felt and loden. Most likely felt balls were as common a toy as the wooden animal figurines found at Trondheim in Norway.

(Right) This felt trader's display of goods shows how many items in everyday use can be made from felt - caps with and without fur trim, socks, shoe soles, toys and lengths of cloth can be seen. Felt was probably more often home made than widely traded.

(Left) These brooches show two different Viking decorative styles. The upper one is copied from a find at Lindholm Hoeje, and shows the Urnes style - a development of the Ringerike style, characterised by fluidly curved lines of varying widths. The Urnes style developed in the 11th century, and did not feature the leaf motifs of other Viking styles. The lower brooch, of Jellinge style, shows the "gripping animal" motif so beloved by the Vikings - an intertwined beast grasps with its claws at its own body or other elements of the motif, such as the frame.

(Left) A caped hood - of which originals have been found at Haithabu and other sites - was the ideal complement for a tunic in bad weather, covering the neck and giving excellent protection; this basic design survived all over Europe for many centuries. A lining of looser-woven cloth was not uncommon; some even had a filling of down between the two layers.

(Below) Reconstructed pendants of both Christian and pagan origin. The *upper row* show the most famous symbol of Viking paganism, the "Thor's hammer", found in a wide variety of styles both abstract (as here) and in the form of realistic hammers. *Bottom left and right* show an interesting intermediate form, reversed here: the cross was actually worn like a Thor's hammer, with the long arm upward. The wolf's mask which shows at the bottom here was the point where a chain or thong was threaded through; the wolf was an important pagan Viking symbol. *Bottom centre* is from an original found at Ribe, Denmark, and depicts a warrior with two birds on his helmet - perhaps dedicated to Odin, or even meant to represent Odin himself; two ravens, two wolves, and an eight-legged horse are among Odin's attributes. The shape hints at the traditional misinterpretation of Viking helmets as "horned".

(Above) *Naalbinding*, a process using a long, thick needle to loop a thread, gives a result not unlike knitting - equally elastic, though slightly thicker. This woman wears a simple linen tunic (presumably used as an undertunic for most of the year) closed at the neck with a small silver pin. The linen is undyed, but the silver bracelet and Thor's hammer, amber necklace and glass beads indicate that she is not poor.

The Viking Woman

The Viking girl was married off early; the fact that an Icelandic law fixes the marrying age for girls at 12 years or more suggests that previously it was not unknown to marry even younger. Questions of relationships between clans played an important part in arranging a marriage, which might cement an important regional alliance. This could bring more influence in the *thing* or assembly, as the two clans were now expected to support each other and to vote together. The bridegroom had to pay a certain amount of money to the father of the bride, as well as proving that he could maintain his wife.

The clothing of the Viking woman was not inferior to that of the men in decoration and material, a fact which shows that they enjoyed high social status. Apart from organising all aspects of the domestic life of the homestead and preparing the meals, the production of clothes was their main task; the necessary techniques, from spinning the yarn to dying and weaving, were mainly practised in the home. If one keeps in mind that a skilled spinner needs approximately ten hours to spin the yarn for one simple tunic, it is clear which task filled most of the woman's time.

(Left & above right) The typical clothing of the Viking wife. Here she wears a linen undertunic, which would be covered in colder weather by a similar woollen tunic. Over all she wears the suspended "apron-skirt", the *hangerock*, here in green with simple red braid edging. The straps attaching the front and back panels of the hangerock are fastened at the shoulder with oval "tortoise" brooches. In wintertime a doubled outer tunic or coat could be worn over the other clothing. Most garments were of ankle length, and some depictions on runestones and jewellery show even longer, trailing dresses. The tunic could be long-sleeved, short-sleeved or sleeveless; a woman's arms were considered a point of attraction, and young women probably preferred to show them off when appropriate. Married women tied their hair up in a knot and covered it with a headscarf; unmarried girls wore it loose, or simply confined with a piece of braid.

This woman has fixed chains of glass beads and amber pendants to her "tortoise" brooches; amber was thought to have magical properties. The centrepiece of the chains is a silver pendant in the style of Jellinge, showing the "gripping animal". Pendants of this type, made in various styles and from gold, silver and bronze, have been found in Scandinavia, England, Ireland and Russia.

The brooches themselves are copied from a find from a woman's grave in Norway. The Jellinge-style pierced decoration shows three interlaced ribbon-shaped beasts with their heads in profile. Most women must have owned a pair of brooches to fasten the hangerock, and many different forms are known; this particular style is rather rare, however.

(Inset left) Among the many duties of the Viking woman was holding the keys for doors and chests. These keys could be hung by a thong or, as shown here, a chain from one of the "tortoise" brooches or a separate brooch. The brass key belongs to a chest; the steel bar-key at right opens a Viking-style padlock. The illustrated scissors are typical for the early Middle Ages; finds range from a few centimetres long, for needlework, to large clippers for shearing sheep, and most are forged from a single piece of steel. Scissors have been found among the belongings of both men and women, but small ones like these appear only in the graves of women.

(Below) Reconstructions of various clasps and brooches worn by the Viking age woman. The concave "tortoise" brooches (*top left & right*) are found nearly everywhere Vikings settled and in all styles. The trefoil (*top centre*) was used to fasten a shawl at the breast. The circular brooches below this are characteristic of Finland, and were also worn in pairs. Animal mask brooches (*bottom left & right*) were associated with Gotland but are also found elsewhere; apart from these all the others are decorated in the Jellinge style.

Daily Life among the Vikings

Slaves and Free Men

Viking society was divided into two groups: free, and slave. Free men were allowed to carry weapons and to own land, which gave them a vote in the *thing* or assembly. These rights were denied to slaves; a slave was the property of his master, who could kill him without punishment as long as he openly admitted it. On the other hand, the master was responsible for the slave's maintenance. A Scandinavian of the Viking age could be a slave by birth, or could descend into slavery. Contemporary authors tell of Vikings who lost home and hearth by gambling, and risked their freedom as the last stake. A woman could also lose her free status if she had relations with a slave.

(Below) For the poorer class the table may rarely have been so well furnished. Hunger was a constant threat; bad harvests were common, and even in good years the crop was only twice the seed. Nevertheless, in good times there were two meals per day from the meat of domesticated cows, sheep, pigs, goats and horses as well as from game such as deer, boar, bear, elk and reindeer. The kitchen garden gave peas, onions, garlic and cabbage; in the woods could be gathered wild cherries, blackberries, raspberries and strawberries, and nuts. The milk of cows and goats was used to make butter and cheese; chicken and geese gave both meat and eggs. Fishing was naturally of great importance to the Viking table; the York excavations even discovered a sort of production line for fish products.

(Above) A Viking child was formally accepted into the family only when the father took it on his knee and called it by its name. Sometimes a family who could not feed a newborn child would abandon it; this was not actually forbidden by law, but was tolerated only if the child was deformed or had not yet been accepted into the family. This infant is certainly in no danger of such treatment; his mother has taken trouble to decorate his clothes and to *naalbind* his socks. The woman's headcloth or wimple shows Anglo-Saxon influence; perhaps this family live in the Danelaw?

Although a slave was not normally allowed to carry weapons there were exceptions to this rule: if a farm was attacked the slaves often fought in its defence at their master's side. Sometimes slaves were given a share of the harvest of the land they worked, and could buy their freedom sooner or later. Even if they did, however, they were hardly better off than before in terms of their daily lives: without any land or capital they had no choice but to hire out as labourers, doing the same work as before. Only slaves who were given a piece of land or a greater sum of money on being set free by their masters had a real chance of improving their lot.

There is no information on how often slaves were set free or bought their freedom, but it happened at least often enough for there to be laws governing the procedure. The Norwegian Frostathing law, written down in the 13th century but probably regularising earlier custom, states that the former slave must prepare a feast for his former master; if the master did not come the seats of honour were left empty. The freed slave and his family owed allegiance to his former master for several generations, but could buy himself out of this duty.

The price for a slave was calculated by age and strength and also, for a female slave, by good looks. A boy cost three goats; a grown man of good health and strength, a pound of silver; and a beautiful woman much more.

The status of a free Viking depended on several things. A landowner was regarded as superior to a landless man serving another; a rich man was superior to a poor one; and a member of an important family counted more than the child of a less influential clan. Relationships were important to the Vikings; having the right connections assured them of help in time of difficulty - the clan was obliged to stand by its members. Fortunes and land were usually inherited by family members so that they did not leave the clan, and if a Viking was forced to sell his land out of need then his relatives had the right to make the first bid.

Women's rights

As already mentioned, marriages were a question of family policy, arranged at a clan level and fixed by contract rather than being solely a private decision for bride and groom. It was only in the Christian period that the Vikings accepted that the bride should be asked for her consent; even so, women's respected social status and their often robust character suggest that forcing a betrothal against a woman's fixed objection might be a perilous business. Originally the bridegroom simply paid a price to the father of the bride; later this sum was passed on to the bride as an inheritance; and finally, the sum was given directly to the bride by the bridegroom. This may have been the reason why daughters received a lesser share of their fathers' inheritance than sons, since their portion was partly settled on marriage.

The fact that marriages were arranged should not be taken to mean that the Viking woman was without rights; the sagas are full of strong and fearless women. The housewife

(Above right) Inside the house the cooking cauldron - usually circular, with a round bottom - was hung on a chain from the roof; out of doors it would hang from a tripod. Note the construction of interwoven, riveted iron straps. In most Viking households the meals were cooked over the fireplace in the hall, at the centre of daily life. Some finds at longhouse sites show evidence of separate rooms being used as kitchens.

(Right) Young boys started to train in the handling of hunting and fighting weapons at an early age. Our little Viking holds a children's shield made from wickerwork, and probably also owns a wooden sword. During winter, when most men stayed close to home, fathers taught their sons all they needed to know to join a raiding party when they were thought ready - perhaps as young as 12, and often by the age of 15 years. However, finds of toys prove that there was still enough time for play.

was the unquestioned ruler of the household, and the keys for all locks which she carried with her were the symbol of her authority. Women had their own money, and could inherit from their parents, husbands, or sons if these died without wife or children. A widow was free to decide whether she wanted to remarry or stay independent.

The *Landnamabok*, a saga of the settlement of Iceland, tells the story of Aud, whose husband died. She then married off her daughters to husbands on the Orkneys and Faroes, and set of on an expedition with 20 free Vikings to settle in Iceland. She seems to have been a historical person around whom many tales were later invented; but the core of all these tales is a free and independent woman taking her fate into her own hands, and respected for it.

Homesteads

Most of the Scandinavian population gained their livelihood by farming, and due to the shortage of good land their steadings were usually scattered quite far apart. Such a farm consisted of a main building sheltering both man and beast; combining the house and the byre had the advantage that in winter the animals' presence would help

(Above left) Viking household goods included tableware and kitchenware made from wood, iron, earthenware and - among the rich - precious metals and imported Frankish glass. Our picture shows several wooden bowls, spoons of wood and horn, pottery cups, a wooden chest, a pan and a knife. The

Vikings also knew the cooper's trade; note the tall cup and the large bowl leaning against the chest, the latter with iron hooping. Small silver cups like the one on the small box were used by the wealthy even before the Viking age, probably for strong fruit wine; the original for this cup was found at Fejö.

(Middle left) Frying pans were made from an iron plate with a light rim riveted onto a long handle; the original of this reconstruction was found in Telemark, Norway. In the

foreground is an eating knife; food was taken with the hands or a spoon, and the knife was used to cut meat. (Forks would not become part of the personal cutlery for centuries.)

(Left) During the winter the Vikings spent their time in carving, among other pastimes, and items of daily use were often decorated in this way - it has been said that "the medieval world abhorred

an undecorated surface". One spoon found at Haithabu features a dragon's-head handle; this collection gives an impression of how personal spoons might be decorated.

(Right inset) The starting positions of the *tafl* game; the dark pieces are the defenders, the larger one in the middle the king. Boards were usually made from wood, pieces from clay, bone, walrus ivory, amber, glass and other materials; there are finds from Trondheim and the Faroes among other places.

(Far right inset) A board near the end of a game; here the corners are not specially marked, suggesting a game by a variant of the rules under which the king only has to reach the edge of the board.

(Left) This re-enactor is pictured in her larder. She stores her supplies in pottery jars, covered with pieces of cloth weighted with glass beads so that no vermin can enter. The housewife was responsible for storage and supervision of the food supplies, and had to plan them so that they would last over the winter. Often the midwinter feast was the last time before the spring thaw that there was enough to eat for everybody.

(Below) Pottery was a desirable traded item, and was even imported from the Rhineland. These pottery bottles are just one example of the large range of crockery wares used in a Viking household for storage, preparation and serving. The Vikings used built-up coil techniques for potting, or hollowed out lumps of clay. The use of a potter's wheel late in the period is proved by a find from Haithabu.

heat the building. In addition to the main building there were often smaller houses for labourers, sheds and workshops; these might be partially dug into the ground so that less material was needed to build them. The construction of the main building depended on the available resources of the area. If timber was plentiful locally then the houses were log cabins. If trees were sparse, a framework of beams

Board games

The Vikings enjoyed games and were enthusiastic gamblers. One group of table-top - *tafl* - games, played on boards of between 7x7 and 19x19 squares, seem to have been very popular with all classes. Many boards and pieces have been found, of qualities from the simplest to the most precious; and one poem refers to the world as "Odin's tafl-board". The rules do not survive completely, but re-enactors have devised a reconstruction which seems to work well.

The attacker, starting at the edges, tries to break the defender's lines and capture his king, which starts in the centre. The defender tries to take his king to safety by moving him onto one of the four corner squares. Players move their pieces alternately, the attacker usually starting. Pieces may be moved horizontally or vertically for any distance, but cannot jump over other pieces of either side. The central square is the "throne" where only the king may rest; all other pieces have to stop before it or move across. The king is the only piece which may move onto one of the corner squares.

Players "capture" the opponent's pieces by surrounding them. A normal piece is captured if the opponent positions one of his pieces on each of two sides, either directly in front and behind or to the left and right; or traps the piece up against the throne or a corner square. The king has to be surrounded from all four sides to be captured.

would be filled in with wickerwork, moss or peat, and clay; and peat would replace logs as the main fuel. Daily life went on around a central fire which served for heating and cooking alike; a Viking's importance in the household could be guessed by the distance of his sleeping place from the fire. The furniture consisted of chests, benches and stools, but it is impossible to say how they were distributed in the house. There is mention of closed off cupboard-beds used by married couples, but privacy for most was probably limited to curtains. For light there were lamps with oil

(Below) Women and men were equally respected, but their areas of life were strictly separate. Spinning, weaving, sewing, embroidery, brewing and cooking were a woman's daily round. Women's graves contain kitchenware, spindles and other household goods, whereas weapons, hunting and fishing items and tools are found in the graves of men. This hard-working young wife, her hair modestly covered by a scarf, wears the simplest clothes and does not own brooches or other jewellery - yet: if her husband gets a place on a successful raiding expedition he will be proud to bring her adornments. Incidentally, one Arab traveller mentions Viking women wearing attractive eye make-up.

(Above) Bread was not a daily food to the Vikings, and gruel was a much more common way of eating cereals. Made without yeast, their unleavened bread could not be stored as it quickly went stale. Apart from barley, the most important baking flour of the Vikings, the *Ringsthula* also mentions thin wheaten bread eaten in the houses of the rich; and a bread find from Sweden includes pea and pine bark flour. Baking was a woman's task at home; this Viking baking his own simple flat loaf is probably on a journey.

or simple tallow dips, later tallow candles, and for the rich, wax candles.

The household goods would include pots of iron, earthenware and soapstone for cooking the two daily meals, iron skewers, earthenware storage pots, wooden or horn spoons, plates and bowls of wood or earthenware, and in the richest households cups of silver or imported glass - although Vikings commonly used a horn for drinking. Knifes were not part of the household goods but belonged to the individual, being carried at all times; they are found in both women's and men's graves. For food there was the meat of wild and domestic animals, fish, beans and peas, greens, nuts, berries, and of course cereals, which were cooked as gruel or hand-milled for flour to bake bread.

Religion
The beliefs of the pagan Vikings - a complex mythological structure which can only be touched upon here - featured a multitude of gods and goddesses divided between two groups, the Aesir and Vanir. The Aesir, who lived in Asgard, were the lords of the world; the Vanir dwelt with them as a mixture of hostages and guests. The supreme

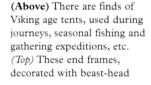

(**Above**) There are finds of Viking age tents, used during journeys, seasonal fishing and gathering expeditions, etc. *(Top)* These end frames, decorated with beast-head carvings, are taken from the tents found with the Oseberg ship. *(Bottom)* These carved frame ends probably represent Odin's ravens Hugin and Munin.

(**Above**) From the sagas we know that the leader or ship's captain used to sleep in a tent when ashore while his crew slept round the campfire in the open. The reconstructed furnishing of this tent is luxurious for the Viking age. Apart from a bedstead, a stool and a sea chest it has a tapestry hanging, and furs are strewn on the floor.

god of the Aesir was Odin, the One-Eyed, the Traveller, the Spear-carrier, the god of heroes; he granted the warrior luck in battle, but every so often he decided to withdraw his favour, in order to gather the fallen hero to his own hall. He knew that one day he would have to face his last battle against the giants and the forces of darkness, and therefore tried to gather all great heroes to the hall Valhalla, to feast and prepare for the final battle - the Ragnarok.

With Odin stood Thor, the god of farmers, ruler of wind and rain, thunder and lightning. Unlike the mysterious Odin, who would do anything and suffer anything to achieve his ends, Thor was honest, straightforward and fearless, though sometimes destructively boisterous; he was viewed with affectionate humour as well as awe. His magical hammer Mjöllnir enabled him to win every fight.

Loki was the element of chaos in the Nordic myths, not only the trickster figure but tirelessly plotting the fall of the gods. Baldur, the purest and most beloved of the gods, died at the hands of a blind innocent tricked into it by Loki. Loki was the father of monsters who would fight against the gods at the Ragnarok: the Fenris wolf, chained up for now at the price of Tyr the Swordsman's sacrificed right hand, but destined to kill Odin; the Midgard serpent, which would die under Thor's hammer in the last fight but would kill him with its venom; Hel, the goddess of the dead, half-woman, half-corpse. . .

Among all these dark apocalyptic visions the lovers Freyr and Freya, brother and sister, stood out. They were Vanir, members of an older and more peaceful race of gods; they did not grant luck in battle, cleverness, success or power, but presided over love and fruitfulness.

We know little about the ritual practices of the heathen Vikings. They did not build temples but did homage to their gods under the open skies; reports of these rituals are often obscure and distorted, not least because they were written largely by Christian monks. Adam of Bremen described the great pagan holy place at Uppsala in about 1070, writing that a major ritual was held every nine years at the spring equinox. During nine days nine male specimens of "every living creature" were sacrificed, and their bodies hung from the trees of the sacred grove, "dogs and horses side by side with men". In the end the number of sacrifices totalled 72.

Other chroniclers also write of human sacrifices as the

75

highest form of homage accorded only to the most important gods; but they claim that Freyr preferred a stallion. This may have been the reason why eating horseflesh was explicitly forbidden to the early Scandinavian Christians; the sacrificed animals were usually eaten by the celebrants in the pagan sacrifice, the meat being believed to be a gift in return for the life which the god had received.

Christian conversion

Scandinavia made contact with Christianity in the early years of the Viking age, and attempts to convert the Vikings were soon made, both at home and in their settlements overseas. These missionaries met with little success, and often enough with martyrdom. However, the Vikings became interested in trading with Christians; and as these equally interested potential trade partners were often forbidden to do business with pagans, a solution was found in the "first blessing". The Viking in question would be told of the Christian beliefs and would receive a blessing; this made him acceptable to Christians for business purposes, but - since he had not been baptised - he could continue to follow the old gods without any problems of concience.

When the Scandinavian countries were united as kingdoms the Christians pursued their usual tactic: they converted the king - for example, Harald Bluetooth, king of Denmark, in 965 - and left it up to him what method he chose to spread the new faith among his people. If he tried to convert them at the point of the sword, then on his soul be it; there were a number of bloody revolts over forced

(Below) It is not unlikely that this girl would have spun the wool for her grey-dyed tunic herself - this was often children's work. She would certainly have known how to cook and bake, and might have had her first practical lessons in weaving. Her parents might already have their eyes open for a suitable boy of influential family to marry her when she reaches her mid-teens.

(Above) This woman checks whether her pot is watertight - it would have been treated with a mixture of dairy products to achieve this. Note the riveted plate construction and the dished lower plate.

Against the cold she wears a leather cap with fur trim, and a caped hood made from cloth of different colours. Although today's re-enactors camp in their tents even in winter, this was not the Viking custom. Parties who had to winter on a strange coast built themselves houses, as told in the Greenland saga.

mass conversion. By c.1000 Norway, Iceland, Greenland, Orkney and the Faroes were all nominally converted.

Only in Iceland did Christianity come peacefully, by a vote of the *allthing*, and at first the old believers were only asked to serve their gods out of sight. Several years later paganism was banned by another vote of the assembly. Nevertheless, the Nordic religion lived on in Scandinavia until the 12th century, Finland becoming the last bastion of the followers of Thor and Odin.

(Above) This well-dressed Viking child enjoys watching some game or competition - perhaps wrestling or skill at arms among the menfolk; perhaps dancing, which was a common part of Viking festivities; or perhaps she is just listening to a *skald* - minstrel - recounting a saga.

(Above left) This highly carved drinking horn *(foreground)* might have been used at Viking feasts; some drinking horns were richly mounted with silver rims and tips. The usual alcoholic drinks were mead, fermented from honey, and a beer made from water and malt only. Viking drinking habits are suggested by the fact that both drinking horns and "turn-over cups" could only be put down when they were empty. A Swedish rune-stone depicts two men at a game, one of them drinking from a horn. The plainer horn in the background represents those blown to sound alarms or pass signals at a distance, in war, hunting or travelling.

(Middle left) Millstones were made from basalt; especially desirable was the black basalt of the Eifel region, imported from the Franks. Analysis of a surviving piece of Viking age bread from Sweden included many small stone fragments, presumably worn off the mill-stone. Preparing large amounts of flour with hand mills like this is tedious and tiring work - which is perhaps part of the reason why the Vikings usually ate gruel, for which the cereals only have to be ground coarsely.

(Left) Leather bottles like these were used to carry water on journeys. To make a bottle like this two pieces of leather were sewn together round the edge and soaked in water; then they were filled with sand, and left to dry. Afterwards the sand was removed and the bottle was filled with wax, which was later melted out again; this makes it completely watertight. Stoppers were of wood or rolled leather.

Traders and Craftsmen

It cannot be repeated too often that although the Norsemen earned their fearsome reputation by looting and killing, Scandinavian traders travelled as widely as raiders throughout this period. Plundering could bring a quick fortune, but only peaceful trade could ensure a steady supply of the desired goods. One of these was Arabian silver, for which the Vikings traded slaves, furs, honey, Norwegian soapstone, wax and weapons - either manufactured in Scandinavia or acquired by force during their long trading voyages. They bartered not only raw materials and finished goods but also tools and "blanks" for later finishing.

Their intensive traffic along all main trading routes between Iceland and the Caspian Sea also brought to northern and eastern Europe luxury goods from western European, e.g. Friesian cloth, black basalt from the Eifel, wine, and glass, as shown by many finds on the sites of the Viking trading centres at Birka, Kaupang, Gotland and Haithabu.

Many traders should more correctly be termed "trader-farmers"; they often owned productive land in Norway, Denmark, Sweden, Iceland or Greenland, as well as settling along the trading routes to found new Viking villages and trading posts where materials were worked or finished.

The first Viking trading centres had already reached their prime by the 9th century, and often came under the special protection of the Norwegian, Swedish and Danish kings. Some of the later centres, like Haithabu, were even founded by kings, because the taxes paid to them by the traders quickly paid for the investment. At Birka, for example, the Swedish king had a three-day option to buy all newly imported goods, ensuring him the best quality and good prices.

Haithabu, one of the main European trading centres between 800 and 1066, counted about 1,000 inhabitants at its peak. Situated close to the Danewerk, the border between Denmark and the Slavs and Franks, it connected western Europe to the trade routes across the Baltic Sea. A nearby port on the North Sea, only 20km (12.4 miles) away, made it unnecessary for Irish and English traders to sail around the Jutland peninsula.

Gotland is supposed to have been the centre of trade in the Baltic Sea. Here archaeologists have found about half of the total number of 20,000 silver coins of Frankish, Arabian and Anglo-Saxon origin recovered in all Scandinavia. The inhabitants of Gotland had extraordinary seafaring skills even by the standards their fellow Vikings and were famous for the high quality of their ships, allowing them to range far afield - and their ships were fast enough to escape pirates. Excavations at Birka near Stockholm in Sweden, a trading city connecting Eastern trading routes with Haithabu in the 8th to 10th centuries, have recovered trade goods including wine, pottery, bronze dishes, weapons and silk, and iron was probably traded here too. However, the main income of

(Left) With luck a Viking trader could earn a fortune within a short time, and he would show his wealth by wearing expensive clothing and jewellery. The quickest and most dangerous way of getting rich was the slave trade with Arab countries; the "stock" was usually collected by force on the way down the Russian rivers to Byzantium. Our trader wears a highly decorated red tunic, and a cloak made of so much cloth that it can be doubled at the shoulders. Mainland European merchants thought Viking traders shifty and untrustworthy, but admired their skills.

(**Above**) Reconstruction of the folding scales used by Viking traders. Although they were probably of Eastern origin, these scales were used from Russia to the British Isles and have been found at Smolensk and Dublin, among other sites. This pair is rather plain; Viking scales were often richly ornamented, with engraved decoration to the pans.

the Birka traders was from the fur trade. Birka had its own assembly; and - as indicated in manuscripts by missionaries who tried to convert the local population - it had connections to Dorestad, a trading centre in today's Netherlands.

In addition to the big trading centres a large number of seasonal market places catered for more local trade; examples are Kaupang in Norway and Moosgard in Denmark. Here goods from England and Ireland - including jewellery, found in many local graves - were bartered for furs, raw hides, walrus tusks and walrus hide ropes with traders from the north. With their capture of York the Danish Vikings also took over an important and long-established Anglo-Saxon trading centre. The Vikings also founded many trading posts in their conquered territories, e.g. Dublin, Limerick, Cork, Wexford and Waterford in Ireland.

Haithabu is thought to be the birthplace of Scandinavian coinage. Silver was the preferred medium of exchange, and coins came to Scandinavia from the Arabs and Franks. Their value was calculated by their weight in silver, so cannot be compared to modern currencies. As already mentioned, the Scandinavians used jewellery such as rings, bracelets, chains and pendants as currency - whole, or cut into pieces. Many Viking hoards found at former trading posts contain large quantities of this "hacksilver" together with foreign silver coins. For example, ten chickens cost a gram of silver; two pounds of grain, 3g; a coat, 12g; a shield and spear, 140g; and a mail shirt, 820 grams.

Wherever traders settled they would be accompa-

(**Above**) Viking trader using his scales to weigh payment. As coins were not yet common in Scandinavia the medium would often be precious metals, which had to be weighed on the spot. The weights used for this were usually transported together with the scales in a special leather bag or box. One such box found in Sweden bears a spell threatening that the "corpse cuckoo" will feed on the body of any thief. Our trader probably hails from the Danelaw, as he wears a "Phrygian" cap in Anglo-Saxon style.

nied by a variety of craftsmen adapting their work to the requirements of the merchants, who supplied the necessary raw materials if they could not be found locally. Viking craftsmen were highly skilled and developed a variety of different styles over the centuries, which can be seen in surviving woodcrafts and jewellery. The styles of Bro, Oseberg, Borre, Jellinge, Mammen, Ringerike and Urnes have been distinguished, evolving from one another and influenced by encounters with non-Scandinavian

(Left) Glass beads were popular as jewellery and as trading goods. To make them, raw glass was melted in pots and cast into sticks. These were then heated again and wrapped around an iron rod to make a bead - it is this step which is illustrated here. To make multi-coloured beads several sticks of different colours were combined or threads of coloured glass were inserted (the technique termed today millefiori). On the board at the upper left we see pieces of raw glass, as they were found in Jutland and Gotland; these were probably imported from northern Italy.

western Europe, heated, drawn into long strings, and then cut into beads; often glass of different colours was mixed to give more colourful beads. Amber from the Baltic Sea and jet from northern England - both believed to have magic properties - were used both for jewellery and for small items like pieces for *tafl* games.

Handicrafts

Many crafts were known in almost every household and practised during the long, hard winters in areas of Viking settlement. Archaeological finds show us women making wool and linen cloth and men making baskets or carving wood and bone. The carving of bone and walrus ivory was very widespread, producing belt buckles, strap ends and combs. Finds of bone combs of Viking origin all over Europe show the popularity of these items; some, carved from deer antlers, are made of several separate pieces - side plates, teeth plates, etc. - and are found with a case also made from antler. (There is

cultures.

The Vikings had blacksmiths, potters, bone and horn carvers, stonemasons, makers of glass beads, bronzesmiths, silversmiths, weavers, dyers, and tanners. To make glass beads - an expensive jewellery in the Viking age - broken glass was imported from

(Right) During the Viking age Scandinavia began to strike coins, which were already in longtime use in western Europe. It was in around 825 that the first coins were minted in Denmark, probably to ease trade with the Franks. The tools shown here include several coin dies and blanks. The blanks were placed between two dies which were struck with a hammer. Sometimes the blanks were so thin that they could only be struck on one side because the punched pattern would go through to the other side (coins of this type are termed bracteats by numismatists).

Smithies, to meet everyday requirements, are found at the majority of Scandinavian farm sites. In Norway blacksmiths' graves have yielded several types of chisel, files, hammers of different sizes, sledge hammers, anvils, and tools for making nails and wire and for casting. One blacksmith was buried with his products including four swords, four spearheads, seven axes, two shield bosses and 13 arrowheads; the pattern-welded and silver-inlaid spearheads show that even complex techniques were known to a simple village blacksmith. Raw iron was stored in the form of bars; another Norwegian find shows 137 of these bars in varying sizes. Large finds of slag prove the production of iron in Norway, and the trade in raw iron and unfinished items like axeheads or sword blades is proved by a find of 12 axeheads with a pine staff threaded through all of them; these were washed ashore in Jutland and are thought to have been produced in Norway. Here one of our blacksmiths is blowing up his furnace with bellows, while the other forms the tang of a knife on his anvil.

an Anglo-Saxon text which complains about the Vikings' unfair advantage in attracting Saxon women due to their vain habit of bathing and dressing their hair every week...)

Almost all households, especially isolated farms, had their own smithies where everyday tools could be forged. Finds prove that tools, wire, nails, hinges and other fittings could be made and repaired in these household smithies. The blacksmith's tools included anvils, hammers, pliers, files, metal shears, chisels and punches as well as special tools to make nails and draw wire. Professional blacksmiths, whether travelling journeymen or established at a trading centre, often specialised in a single technique such as making mail or weapons.

(Below) The original of this hearthstone is thought to be from Norway or southern Sweden. The face is assumed to represent the god Loki, who was the god of fire among other things and therefore had a special relationship to blacksmiths. The lines through his mouth are an allusion to a tale in which Loki got his mouth sewn closed because of a lost bet.

(Left) Fishing was a major source of food for the Scandinavian peoples. The population of Haithabu are known to have had more than 20 different sorts of fish on the menu, including both fresh water and salt water varieties. Fish was preserved by salting, drying or smoking, which allowed it to be traded. Fishing was performed by throwing nets from small boats or, if local tidal streams made it feasible, by setting nets across the waterway to catch fish at low water. Bigger fish were also speared from the banks of the rivers.

(Below) Fishing equipment, including all the tools necessary to spin yarn and to make nets - spindles, spools of thread, shuttles and scissors. Hooks were made from wood, horn or metal, and several were fixed to one line. At right foreground are five weights as used to hold down nets which spanned rivers. Little fishing kit has survived from the Viking age, but textual references prove that fishing was practised with rod and line as well as with nets, at sea and on the lakes and rivers.

(Above) This net made from a forked branch is used for landing fish caught with rod or line. In the left background stands a small lidded wooden tub of the type used in Scandinavia for holding all kinds of small odds and ends.

Evidence of metal casting has been found by archaeologists at all major trading posts. The variety of produced items ranges from rare and expensive gold and silver jewellery to cheap mass produced wares. The metal was melted in a charcoal furnace powered by bellows. The piece was first formed from wax and this master was embedded in clay. When the clay mould had hardened the wax was melted out and the resulting space was filled with molten metal

(Below) Bone and antler were much used for everyday items. The bones used included those of whales, from which large, flat pieces could be cut. The deer antlers used for carving did not have to be from hunted game, but could be simply collected in the forest after the annual cast. The tools pictured here are suitable for carving bone and wood: saw, whetstones, hammer and knives.

(Above) Comb carved from bone *(bottom centre)*, plane, whetstone, knives, file and auger. The bone carver used the auger to drill fixing holes into belt buckles and strap ends; to make an openwork carving he would first drill a hole through his material and then continue carving from there. The comb illustrated has a fitted case made similar to the comb side plates. Combs of this type are found all over Europe, and were one of Scandinavia's main exports.

(Below) Some established trading posts even boasted small huts which new arrivals could rent for a time; but normally the trader would simply raise his tent, or sell his goods directly from the ship. Here a traveller has set out his various trade goods including furs, shoes, blankets and weapons; his wife guards the stock while he is off scouring the camp for customers. The tent form is typical for the Viking age: two triangular frames linked by three parallel horizontals, the canvas fixed to the frame with ropes. This type of tent was originally found on the Oseberg ship.

- the so-called lost wax method. When the metal was cold the clay was broken off, and the piece finished by filing, adding pins, gilding, etc. Simpler items could themselves be pressed into clay to make moulds for mass produced castings.

Viking craftsmen were very inventive, always developing new products, styles and methods of production. But it often took a hundred years or more for a new technique to be spread across the borders of the region by travelling craftsmen and traders, so technological progress was slow. Indeed, craftsmen often deliberately held back from spreading new inventions so as to avoid competition for their wares.

(Above) Every item seen here was made from bone, horn or antler. The list ranges from weaving tablets, needles, combs, rings, needlecases and a "weaving sword" to strap ends, jewellery and dice. Finds have also included bone beads, belt buckles, buttons, chess pieces, knife handles, cloak pins, tools for smoothing cloth, sword cross-guards, and chest panels for fitting into a metal frame-work. In the early medieval period all Europeans made from bone the thousand and one small items of daily necessity which today we make from plastic.

(Below left) This craftsman owns a tool which was relatively rare in Viking times: a saw. The only craft for which this was absolutely necessary was comb-carving; other craftsmen could make do with various straight blades. The chests in front of him were used both as sea chests and rowing benches by travelling Vikings, which accounts for the trapezoid-shaped sides; they could be fastened with a padlock.

(Below) A woman's sewing kit. Pins and needles were made from bone and would only become smooth with regular use. Because needles broke easily, especially at the points, the Vikings made needle cases from long bones - that illustrated here was made from the foreleg of a lamb.

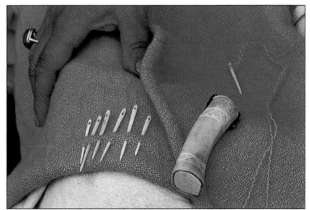

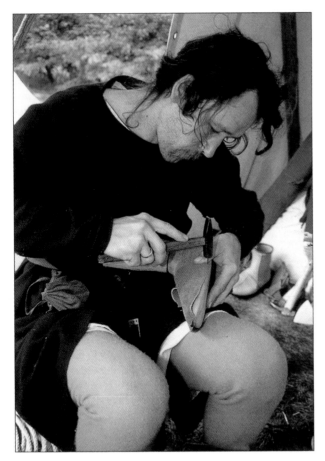

(Above) On the farm shoe-making was a homecraft, but there is plentiful evidence that at the major centres it was a commercial trade performed by specialists; Haithabu and Birka have provided many finds of shoes and leather offcuts. Our shoemaker is putting the upper leather of a shoe onto a last to make it fit the form of a foot.

(Above) The shoemaker's wife is perforating the edges of the sole to make it easier to sew to the upper. Footwear of this period were "turn-shoes", i.e. the seams were on the inside. Although fitted only with a simple leather sole these shoes are warm enough to be worn in winter if provided with a felt inner sole; they also give a good grip.

(Right) Various reconstructed shoes of the 7th to 11th centuries. *(Top left)* High boot, as originally found at Haithabu. *(Centre, left to right):* Decorated, side-laced ankle boot from Starja Ladoga; shoe from Haithabu; ankle-high shoe from Norwich, the flaps to be fastened with toggles. *(Bottom left to right):* Similar to Norwich example, the original found at York; decorated shoe found at Ballymacob; shoe from Middleburg, lined with lambswool. Varying shapes and decoration suggest that shoes, as well as clothing, were influenced by local custom and styles, although it is quite unrealistic to speak of "fashion" in the modern sense.

Runestones

The Vikings had an oral tradition; their system of runic characters was originally used mainly for magical inscriptions and for the shortest texts. It was only later contact with Christianity which introduced literacy to Scandinavia. The interpretation of pagan Viking culture is thus a problem for historians, as there are few written documents.

Runestones are among the most important textual finds of the Viking age because - in contrast to the major texts such as the *Landnamabok, Iceland Saga* and *Prose Edda*, which were written down after the actual Viking age to record tales which had only been passed down orally up to then - runestones were genuinely contemporary. They were carved by the Vikings themselves as a permanent record of events, as memorials to the dead, or to make other types of formal public statement.

Of course, even the analysis of all known surviving runestones would not give us a complete picture of Viking culture; but each stone illuminates some small aspect of a society which we would otherwise know only in the words of its enemies and victims.

For example, a Viking woman is recorded as setting up a runestone in memory of her missing son: this shows us that she could undertake an independent, public project and be reported as its initiator, and that she was wealthy enough to pay the craftsman to carve the inscription. Moreover, in times when men disappeared on raiding parties never to return, the setting up of a memorial stone may have marked an official declaration of death for inheritance purposes. The circumstances of a violent death, which are often set down on such stones, also throw light on the sense of honour governing behaviour among peoples who were often dismissed by (not unnaturally) biased foreigners as barbaric and treacherous.

Their reputation for anarchic individualism is also contradicted by the number of runestones set up to record a public service. In Scandinavia there was no centrally organised road construction, and the individual was responsible for maintaining the roads crossing his land. A Viking taking the trouble or expense to build a bridge or a length of new road would set up a runestone so that the public knew who deserved the credit. (The carver of the stone itself also usually recorded his name.)

The runic alphabet

The interpretation of runestones is made especially difficult by the fact that the alphabet of 16 runes used by the Vikings does not have enough characters to cover all the sounds of the Nordic tongue. A single rune served for several sounds; and, as there was no standard notation but every word was written phonetically, a single word can have several rune notations - and these are often influenced by dialects. Moreover, double consonants were often contracted to a single mark; e.g. if one word ended with N and the next word started with N, only a single N-rune was marked.

To add to the difficulty, runes were often integrated into pictorial carvings; the most typical are snakes and dragons with the runes engraved along their entwined bodies. If the artist had miscalculated the length of the text the remaining runes were squeezed somewhere in between - and the chaos for the translator is complete. It is hardly surprising that translations of the same text by different scholars often include not only slight differences in wording, but completely different meanings, neither one of which is obviously the less convincing.

The runestones do clearly demonstrate that the Vikings, despite their oral culture, were by no means completely illiterate. There is no sense in setting up a public announcement which none of your neighbours can understand. Those who went to the trouble and expense of erecting them presumably expected that a considerable number of passers-by would know how to read them, or would know somebody else who could. However, neither such stones - nor the carved sticks which were used to pass

The assembly

The assembly - *thing* - was the heart of the democracies which governed Scandinavia during the early Viking age. It was usually held annually, and was the central authority within a region. Every free man could vote; all important questions of public affairs were discussed, laws were decided and pronounced, and lawsuits settled. Above the regional assembly there was a superior assembly, settling differences between regions.

In Iceland this was the *allthing*, held at Thingvellir for 14 days during the summer. Together with its administrative and judicial functions it also served as a market and meeting place for the people of the more remote areas. Meetings were held among the 36 Icelandic leaders under the authority of the "law-speaker", elected for three years and presiding on the "law stone". Here the regional leaders would discuss all outstanding matters; and when cases came to judgement each leader named one judge, usually a man renowned for wisdom.

A legal decision by an assembly - which in the early years had to be unanimous - was binding, on pain of outlawry; any who defied it could be killed without consequences. This threat was enough to enforce the judgement - the Vikings had no "executive forces". The winning party to a lawsuit could claim compensation, but had to collect it themselves. In questions of honour or revenge the plaintiff could also claim the right of trial by combat, which was fought in front of the assembly.

Viking justice was distinct from contemporary mainland European systems in that its main aim was individual compensation, not the revenge of society as a whole. A manslaughter could be settled by paying *wergeld*, "man-money", the amount being set by the assembly. It brought no dishonour on the family to accept this money, and blood feuds were only pursued in cases when the culprit could not pay, or if the circumstances of the killing were disgraceful, e.g. a murder committed from behind. To kill another man's slave was simply property damage, and the culprit had to refund the slaveowner.

runic inscriptions from hand to hand - were a suitable medium for recording the details of personal or family history at any length. For such a purpose the ancient oral tradition of heroic poetry, passed down the generations by bards, was both more practical and more appropriate to the Viking character - they would have had little sympathy for the Roman historian Tacitus' declared goal of recording the cold facts "with neither anger nor enthusiasm".

(**Right**) All over northern Europe archaeologists have identified the runestones used by Vikings as a permanent record of some public announcement or important private event. After the runic characters were chiselled into the stone they were often coloured to make them stand out; and sometimes words were distinguished from one another by the use of alternating colours. One of the most famous and eloquent examples is a marble lion statue which used to stand in the Greek port of Piraeus near Athens. It bears two lines of a Norse runic inscription, now almost completely worn away, but once scratched into the stone as graffiti by some Viking mercenary fighting for Byzantium - a vandal, but not an illiterate one. . .

Personal names

The Viking system of names was easily understandable. A newborn child was given a first name by his or her parents - e.g. Olaf, Svein, Ragnar, Harald, etc. The second name was that of the father, with the suffix "-son" or "daughter" - e.g. Eric son of Haakon was Eric Haakonsson. (This system survives even today in Iceland, viz. the Icelandic-born British broadcaster Magnus Magnusson.) Many Vikings received a more or less flattering nickname during their lifetime, which distinguished between people of the same name. There may have been many Harald Sigurdssons, but only one Harald Sigurdsson "the Hard"; and for famous men this additional name often took the place of the patronymic, so that sagas speak simply of "Harald *Hardrada*", "Olaf the Saint", "Ivar the Boneless", etc.

The Normans

The major Christian power at the time of the emergence of the Vikings from their northern mists was the so-called Carolingian Empire. Founded in the mid-8th century by the Frankish King Pepin, this was led to its greatest prestige by King Charles the Great ("Charlemagne"), who was crowned Holy Roman Emperor in 800. From its heartland between the Rhine and Meuse it had spread to embrace most of continental western Europe, from the Atlantic to Bohemia and from the North Sea to Rome.

Trading connections between Scandinavia and the Franks via Friesia on the North Sea coast predated the first Norse raids on the empire; but an attack by King Godfred's Danish Vikings on Friesia in 810 started a plague which would afflict the continent for a century and a half. From the death of the Emperor Louis I in 840 central authority weakened; from 887 the empire formally split into French

and German kingdoms; Frankish military preparedness decayed, at exactly the time when it was needed most.

In 834 Dorestad was devastated; in 841, Rouen; in the years which followed cities far up the Garonne and the Seine were plundered, among them Paris in 845, 857 and 886. Like the Anglo-Saxons before them, the Franks under Charles "the Bald" tried to buy peace by paying *danegeld* to the Vikings; just the first of 13 payments recorded between 845 and 926 amounted to 3500kg (7,700lbs) of silver. Predictably, these subsidies only bought a short respite; Hamburg was plundered by Vikings in 845, Cologne in 862/863, and Trier in 882. Neither was the Atlantic coast

(Left) Most speculation about the early Norman fighting man is based on the Bayeux Tapestry depicting the conquest of England in 1066. Norman knights are shown heavily armoured with nasal helmets, mail hauberks with coifs, and carrying the long kite- shaped shield which became common in the 11th century. The 11th century ringmail hauberk was knee-length or even longer, split front and back for riding, with sleeves at least to the elbow; there is also some evidence for mail leggings to protect riders' legs.

(Below) While light troops like bowmen, and some poorer mercenaries, still went into battle wearing tunics or, at best, padded gambesons, the bulk of the battle line would now have been equipped with ringmail. We can assume that William the Conqueror provided at least his own household troops with this expensive piece of equipment. Although some of these re-enactors still wear the old-fashioned shorter corselet, the second and third from the left show the longer, split-skirted defence. Their helmets are a variety of different spangenhelms, all with nasal protection. The Saxon *huscarls*, too, would have worn ringmail and helmets, and many were armed with the long Danish axe. On the Bayeux Tapestry most Norman knights are armed with swords and spears, only a few carrying axes and saxes.

of the empire safe: in 835 an island monastery in the mouth of the Loire was plundered, and ten years later the Vikings rowed up the river to pillage Nantes.

In the middle years of the 9th century the Christian inhabitants of the empire suffered repeated massacre, pillage and destruction, to the extent that large areas of the Frankish kingdoms became depopulated by mass flight. Although the empire could field the first seeds of what would become the classic heavy armoured cavalry of western Europe, it was weakened by the collapse of central authority; by a strained exchequer after it ceased its earlier wars of expansion and conquest; and by the simultaneous distraction of a Moslem threat from the south.

Payment of danegeld developed into the actual ceding of Frankish territory for Viking settlement. In the mid-9th century the island of Walcheren in Friesia was granted to the Danes in return for protection against further Viking attacks. In 911 Rolf, the leader of a Viking army which had plundered northern France, was granted the area between the rivers Bresle, Epte, Avre and Dives as a fief from King Charles III "the Simple" of the West Franks, in return for his sworn loyalty and military support. Rolf converted to

(Left) Although many variations of detail are probable, the most typical helmet for the era of the Norman Conquest was probably the spangenhelm with nasal, as depicted in many period sources; its construction would have been quicker and cheaper than a helmet "drawn" over a stake by hammering a single sheet of metal. This reconstructed example is worn with a close mail coif which leaves only the face exposed, though protected by the broad nasal.

Hastings 1066

On 28 September 1066 the invasion fleet of William of Normandy reached Pevensey in south-east England, and landed not only infantry spearmen and bowmen but armoured cavalry and their horses. The news reached the Anglo-Saxon King Harold hundreds of miles to the north where, at Stamford Bridge on 25 September, he had defeated and killed Harald Hardrada. Within 14 days Harold had marched his tired, weakened army south to defend his throne from this new threat. On 14 October the two armies met at Senlac Hill near Hastings, close to the present site of Battle Abbey.

Ironically, it was Harold's all-infantry army, 6,000-7,000 strong, which more closely echoed those of the Vikings. Around his banners his *huscarls* or elite household troops formed a shield wall several ranks deep; around them on the hilltop were arrayed the *fyrd*, the Anglo-Saxon emergency levy of all free men. Harold had seen what Norman cavalry could do while accompanying William on an earlier continental campaign; the hilltop position he chose was intended to counter this threat. William's troops were indistinguishable from any other Frankish army of the day; he had perhaps 3,500 Norman professional soldiers, supported by about the same number of Bretons, Flemings and other mercenaries, and up to 2,000 of the total were mounted. William deployed his troops in three blocks, the Normans in the centre flanked by the Bretons and Flemings.

The first clash took place in the late morning, when a Breton attack was bloodily pushed back by the Saxon fyrd; but the Norman cavalry succeeded in separating the pursuing Saxons from their main body by a flank attack, inflicting heavy loss. At noon William attacked again; again the Normans had to withdraw, and William was unhorsed - but it is suggested that the retreat was partly deliberate, to lure the Saxon militia into another unwise pursuit. Another attack in the afternoon cost the duke a second mount and still brought no decision; but by now the dwindling Saxon ranks were definitely tiring.

The decisive moment came in the late afternoon with the fourth attack, when William's bowmen dropped arrows into the Saxon formation from a high angle, followed by an all-out assault directly at the defenders of Harold and his banner. This proved successful; traditionally Harold is said to have been hit in the eye by an arrow, others say that he was cut down by Norman cavalry, and others still that he was carried from the battlefield alive but died shortly afterwards. Either way, his banner faltered and fell; word of his death spread through his exhausted army, and the formation broke at last. The Normans pursued the fleeing fyrdmen, but with the falling dusk they were called back after a troop had been ambushed and cut down.

William was crowned king of England in London on 25 December, though it would be several years before the last pockets of Saxon resistance were stamped out. His extraordinarily ambitious invasion and his hard-won victory were to prove perhaps the most decisive turning-point in British history, changing the direction of national development forever.

Christianity, taking the name Rollo, and Normandy served as a buffer zone against further Viking attacks. His son, Duke William I, received further territory.

The new settlers from Scandinavia mixed with the existing Gallo-Roman and Germano-Frankish strains. This was achieved more readily in the central region around Rouen than on the coastal fringes, and Normandy was not finally unified until 1047, when a rebellion by coastal lords was put down by Duke William II "the Bastard" and King Henry I of France. Henry's attempts to conquer his over-mighty Norman vassal in 1054 and 1057 failed, cementing William's position.

The death of the Anglo-Saxon King Edward "the Confessor" in 1066 sparked the events leading to a Norman expansion all over Europe. Duke William had been promised the throne of England by his kinsman Edward; when his claim was usurped by the great Saxon magnate Earl Harold Godwinsson, William landed an invasion force on the south coast of England on 28 September 1066. A competing attempt was made by "the last of the Vikings", King Harald Hardrada of Norway, who landed on the Yorkshire coast. Harold Godwinsson defeated the Viking army, then force-marched south to meet the Norman threat. The last Saxon king of England was killed and his army defeated at Hastings on 14 October; the Norman duke - descended over a few generations from the pagan Viking raider Rolf, but now a Frankish nobleman in all but name - was crowned King William I of England on Christmas Day in Westminster Abbey.

From the mid-11th century their extraordinary energy, hardihood, greed and quarrelsomeness spread the rule of restless Norman barons across a great part of Europe. Though they had long forgotten their ancestral culture, men who could trace their paternal blood to Rolf's plunderers seized power as far south as Sicily and the Balkans; Norman knights put an end to Byzantine predominance in the Mediterranean, and launched the First Crusade in the Holy Land. A new age of the world was growing out of the long confusion of post-Roman Europe; and with every generation the Vikings receded further into heroic legend.

(Above) This Norman re-enactor can be seen to wear a gambeson beneath his mail - a necessary defence against the impact of blows ("blunt trauma"), since the rings themselves only give protection against cuts. Without padding to cushion and spread the impact , the crushing force of, e.g., a Danish axe - which could actually dismember men and horses - would still break major bones, and force split mail rings deep into the flesh beneath.

(Left) Period depictions show what re-enactors have learned for themselves: that the only comfortable way to carry a mail shirt is slung on a pole through the sleeves. The special dynamics of the distribution of its weight also make a long hauberk very difficult to put on or pull off without help. Note here the split upwards from the hem to allow riding, and an added flap of mail on the chest which was laced upwards to protect the face.

(Above) The so-called "kite" shield, which slowly replaced the old round type throughout much of Europe during the 11th century, covered the whole front of the bearer's body from chin to ankle, with a slightly dished cross-section to give even better protection. It was made from several glued planks, and probably covered with leather and rimmed with leather or iron to stop the wood from splintering. Contemporary depictions show shields both with and without bosses. Shield decorations on the Bayeux Tapestry feature the Christian cross as well as dragons, griffons and floral motifs.

(Above right) The long shield was carried by a number of leather straps that could be gripped in different ways to lift and move the shield. The weight of the shield could be transferred to the shoulders by a sling. Although it is most likely that the shield was carried vertically in the fight, pictures also show warriors holding it horizontally. There are no 11th century finds of such shields, and reconstructions are based on contemporary pictures and 13th century originals. To make carrying the shield more comfortable padding has been added here to the inside surface under the leather straps.

(Right) A slight variation of the shield grips; and detail of a reconstructed Norman sword. These were longer than their Viking predecessors; often used from horseback, they had to give a longer reach. The larger crossguard and pommel, which were slid onto the tang of the sword and welded in place, balance the weight of the longer blade around its centre of gravity, making it still controllable with one hand.

(Above & right) Three stages in donning the typical Norman head protection. Some kind of padded cap is the necessary first step, made from thick woollen cloth, leather or linen; it performs the same protective function as the gambeson beneath the mail corselet, and also stops the wearer's hair getting caught in the mail coif or hood worn over it. In the 11th century this was already seen attached permanently to the hauberk, but separate coifs were also in use. The lower face is then covered with a square flap of mail, attached to the breast along its lower edge and - presumably - laced up to the coif. Finally the helmet is put on, this example being the typical European spangenhelm with nasal.

Norman Cavalry

At the decisive battles of Val-és-Dunes in 1047 and Hastings in 1066 the Normans successfully deployed their knights as cavalry. The hard core of William the Conqueror's army can rightfully be called "knights", as the feudal system was already entrenched: a pyramid of mutual obligation based on sworn loyalty and land tenure, the land grant providing the revenue which equipped the vassal knight to fulfill his military duties when summoned by his lord, and freeing him from most mundane daily concerns.

During his childhood the future Norman man-at-arms was trained for war both formally and by hunting from horseback in rough terrain. By about 12 years of age the son of a knight was familiar enough with the handling of horses and weapons to begin his duties as a squire, the servant/apprentice of a knight. He might be knighted by his lord at around the age of 21; if an elder son, he might marry and settle down on his family land; if landless, he might take paid service with a lord. It was this type of young men who followed William to England in 1066 to seek their fortunes.

The cavalry was probably deployed in groups of 25 to 50 riders; and during the early Middle Ages these units operated with much less co-ordination, once launched into battle, than would satisfy later ideas of "command and control". The individual fighting man would use his weapon according to his own judgement. The spear was probably used for stabbing both overarm and underarm, rather than levelled for the co-ordinated frontal charge of later periods.

Cavalry were mainly used for flank attacks, or for exploiting gaps hacked in the enemy formations by the infantry, to turn a moment of wavering into rout and defeat. Frontal attacks on an unbroken enemy force would be costly; the unarmoured horses were vulnerable to arrows, and at close range to javelins and spears. It is, in any case, almost impossible to make a horse charge right into a standing formation like a shield wall; at Hastings the Norman cavalry would have been reduced to riding up and down in front of the Saxon shields, stabbing down with their spears or throwing them like javelins in attempts to break the line.

Once the fighting opened out, however, a horse's herd instincts would make it run with the others, and with foot soldiers; and once the enemy were put to flight cavalry were ideal for pursuing the fugitives to prevent them from rallying, cutting them down left and right. Riders were also used for reconnaissance, as foragers to commandeer supplies, and as raiders to ravage the enemy's territory.

Training and maintenance of war horses was costly, and cavalry were precious to a commander; therefore they were usually held back behind the foot troops out of range of missile weapons, and only deployed when they were sure of a decisive effect.

(**Above**) Seen from behind, our cavalryman shows the necessity for the central splits from the hem of the mail hauberk - they allow the mail to fall smoothly over the thigh when the rider is in the saddle. Some knights are also shown wearing protective mail leggings. Note the neckguard of the helmet; some images in the Bayeux Tapestry show this type of rear bar protection. The clothing of our man-at-arms is simple, consisting of a tunic, trousers, leg wrappings and ankle-length leather shoes.

(**Below**) This spangenhelm has no brow band; the rivets around the bottom presumably secure an adjustable leather lining cap. The helmet has cheekpieces, a frontal nasal and a similar bar at the back to protect the neck. Helmets with exactly this combination of features have not been found, but each can be proved for our period, so the existence of such a helmet is likely.

(**Left & inset**) The 11th century Norman cavalryman probably did not look very different, in terms of clothing and armour, from any other fully equipped northern European warrior. Judging by the Bayeux Tapestry he was armed with both lance and sword (though there is an isolated image of an armoured rider with a bow). His armour consisted of helmet and ringmail hauberk, and a slung kite-shaped shield protected his whole left side down to the foot. Such evidence as we have suggests that shield motifs at this date were purely decorative; the complex medieval system of heraldic identification had not yet appeared.

When fighting he controlled his horse with one hand and by the pressure of his legs and spurs. The detail shows the stirrup, here reconstructed with a leather socket laced on for resting the ferrule of the lance while riding. Simple iron spurs of the era recovered by archaeologists are straight with small pointed tips.

Sources & select bibliography

Exhibition catalogues:
Wikingermuseum Haithabu: *Schaufenster einer frühen Stadt,* Hildegard Elsner; 2nd edition, Schleswig (1994)
Museum für Vor- und Frühgeschichte Berlin: *Wikinger, Waräger, Normannen;* Berlin (1992)

Other publications:
The Anglian Helmet from Coppergate, Dominic Tweddle; London (1992)
Viking Scotland, Anna Ritchie; London(1993)
Regia Anglorum Member's Handbook, Ben Levick et al.; Bristol (1992)
Wikinger, John D.Clare; Nürnberg (1991)
Wikinger, Susan M. Margeson & Peter Anderson; Hildesheim (1994)
Das Leben der Wikinger, James Graham Campbell; München (1993)

Chronicles of the Vikings, R.I.Page; London (1995)
Die Wikinger, Robert Wernick; Eltville (1992)
Die Wikinger; 3rd edition, Burkhard-Verlag Ernst Heyer; Essen (1992)
The Norman Knight, Christopher Gravett & Christa Hook; Osprey Warrior Series, London (1993)
The Viking Hersir, Mark Harrison & Gerry Embleton; Osprey Warrior Series, London (1993)
The Vikings, Ian Heath & Angus McBride; Osprey Elite Series, London (1985)
The Normans, David Nicolle & Angus McBride; Osprey Elite Series, London (1987)
Hastings 1066, Christopher Gravett; Osprey Campaign Series, London (1992)
Byzantine Armies, Ian Heath & Angus McBride; Osprey Men at Arms Series, London (1979)